Forecast: Disaster

The Future of El Niño

Henry F. Porter

A Dell Book

Published by
Dell Publishing
a division of
Bantam Doubleday Dell Publishing Group, Inc.
1540 Broadway
New York, New York 10036

ISBN: 0-440-22661-9

Printed in the United States of America

Published simultaneously in Canada

January 1999

10 9 8 7 6 5 4 3 2 1

OPM

For Amy and 506

Contents

A change in the weather is known
to be extreme. . . .
—Bob Dylan

1

El Niño Strikes

It was, as they say, a dark and stormy night. The latest in a recent spate of thunderstorms was punishing the small town built along the Cuyama River, some twenty-five miles from where it flows into the Pacific. Right now, the Cuyama was flowing toward the mighty ocean with considerably more force than usual.

Swollen by the rains, the river raged over its banks to engulf all alongside and before it in a torrent of water turned a rich chocolate brown from the tons of earth and debris it had consumed. Not far from this surge of muddy water, a lone squad car sped through the night, its lights flickering through the downpour. Officers Rich Stovall and Britt Ervine were hastening to a distress call, one of the many that had crackled across the police band during the long evening. On the way to aid the storm's victims, they became victims themselves.

Unknown to the pair, the highway just ahead ended with deadly abruptness, the roadway washed away by the river. Unable in the dark night to see that the highway became a sheer drop to the roiling mud below, Officers Stovall and Ervine plunged into the chilly waters where, trapped inside their squad car, they drowned. Rescue teams later dug the car out of a sandbar, where it had been left buried upside down by the water's recession. Though two fortunate motorists survived similar experiences, the two officers were not the only victims of the river's terrible strength, as two others died and another, missing, was feared dead as well.

Other tales of weather-related tragedy and disaster were told throughout California during that week in which California first felt the wrath of winter 1998. The storms claimed a number of lives and gave much of the state its wettest February in history. The weather shattered precipitation records from Los Angeles to San Francisco and battered California's gorgeous—and substantially developed—coastline. In the coastal town of Pacifica, twenty miles north of San Francisco, houses marched inexorably toward a precipice dug by a fusillade of Pacific waves. Some toppled into the waves below, dream homes lost to the same forces that had granted them such dramatic vistas.

The worst damage, however, came from the rains, which caused mud slides throughout the state in towns such as Laguna Beach. Hillsides shed tons of earth that the rain had saturated to the point of liquefaction. Those unfortunates in the mud's path were shoved downhill under a force witnesses likened to a freight train. Mud slides claimed several lives in California that week and left many more homeless. Hospitals filled with the stunned, muddied victims of the storms. Meanwhile, a giant sinkhole was consuming Interstate 15—cars, pavement, and trees alike sliding into its ever-widening maw. The week left Californians dazed and mourning, many searching for the strength to rebuild lives and work lost so quickly to the weather's fury.

Residents of central Florida, though three thousand miles removed from California's wet misery, found themselves in a similar state of weather-induced woe. The day before the worst of the California mud slides, the most severe and deadly series of tornadoes in Florida's history smashed the area surrounding Kissimmee. The twisters struck in a part of Florida where they were rare, and when they did appear, they tended to be relatively small affairs.

The tornadoes that struck on February 22, however, were titanic in their force. They touched down

seemingly by ordination to crush rows of houses in
suburban developments while sparing homes just
across the street. In trailer parks struck by the twisters, though, the destruction was nearly universal. The
tornadoes picked up mobile homes as if they were
toys, tossing them great distances, all too many times
along with their inhabitants. Parks such as Morning-
side Acres came to symbolize the tragedy. Poignant
indeed was the spectacle of survivors facing twisted
piles of metal in which they had lost their homes,
their generally modest possessions, possibly a wife or
an infant son.

Rescue teams and police K-9 units dug for days
through heaps of rubble at first in a desperate search
for survivors and then, as time wore on cruelly, in a
grim excavation of the dead. The tornadoes—striking
a region unaccustomed to such forceful storms, and
earlier in the season than is generally the norm—
caught many by surprise, leading to a reevaluation of
tornado warning measures. The spasm of atmospheric
violence killed forty-two people and inflicted millions
of dollars' worth of damage upon a state left bereft
and grieving in its wake. Central Florida, like so
much of California, was declared a federal disaster
area.

What was going on here? Was there a connection
between these far-distant meteorological tragedies?
As everyone by now knows, they were but the beginning of a season of calamity for the United States.

And the United States was neither the only, nor the first, nor even the hardest hit of nations by the brutal extremes of weather felt throughout the globe in 1997 and 1998. In Australia, crops withered in dry, hot earth under a killing sun; in Brazil, farmers raced to bring in a tobacco harvest before it rotted from the ceaseless rain. The western United States suffered its wettest winter while the East reveled in its warmest. Drought-fed forest fires consumed thousands of acres in Indonesia and Southeast Asia; in Peru and Ecuador, miles of the Pan-American Highway became the bed of a huge new lake created by a seemingly endless parade of storms. Strange weather, often tragic in its consequences, seemed the rule during a sustained period of broken meteorological records and wholesale devastation.

When the late February mud slide in California occurred within a day of the worst tornadoes in Florida's history, a connection was almost universally drawn between the two, as if they were bank heists linked by a common perpetrator with a variety of modi operandi. The verdict was swift and the culprit, as all manner of media proclaimed, was something called El Niño, a planet-wide weather phenomenon far reaching in its consequences, about which many were hearing for the first time.

By early spring, "El Niño" had seemingly usurped cyber-anything as the nation's most tired catch phrase. The meteorological event had been dragged out and dissected from all angles and blamed for a laundry list of travesties. It became nightly fodder for television talk show monologues, the stuff of Top Ten List compilers' dreams. El Niño even entered the realm of politics, providing fancy for the pens of political cartoonists who envisioned, among other permutations, United States Attorney General Janet Reno transformed to "El Reno." By midsummer, its influence could be felt along the breadth of the zeitgeist, from its place as a prominent tag line in the genre movie send-up *Mafia!* to its inspirational role in the title and cover art of the underground CD release *Worlds on Fire* by rock avant-gardist Jade Hoye.

The El Niño hype, ironically, often obscured the fact that the hype was to a large degree justified. This El Niño had received a great deal of advance billing in the summer and fall of 1997 as the "storm of the century" (a misleading phrase, as we shall see). When the United States made it through the beginning of the phenomenon—November, December, and January—relatively unscathed, many wrote off the forecasts as empty scientific talk. El Niño's pernicious effects were in fact already taking hold in South America and Southeast Asia, but it was not until the cataclysm of late February that Americans became convinced that the phenomenon was for real.

Beginning with the events of late February, media coverage of El Niño gave much more space and time to pictures of devastation and interviews with battered survivors of the system's wrath than it did to explanations of what, exactly, El Niño is; of how it is that the United States can be affected by warm water thousands of miles away, off the coast of Peru; of when in the past El Niño had struck and what its effects had been; of how scientists have been engaged in a century-long race to understand the phenomenon so as to provide us with a better warning of its approach; and of how El Niño fits into the world's climate and its dangerous state at the end of the twentieth century. This is not to blame the media, who must continually deliver fresh stories to the public. It is often simply not possible to provide more than cursory background to news stories, especially when the stories are fraught with human drama and a glimpse into the awesome force of nature, as were those that came out of California and central Florida in February of 1997.

But viewing El Niño as we have, as a relentless stream of disasters amid forecasts of further doom, has given us only a series of snapshots of its effects. Like photos in a family album, these views of El Niño can be weighted with strong feeling—the misery of one who has survived a mud slide only to hear that a loved one has not, the feeling of helplessness one feels upon learning that El Niño's warm ocean temperatures are killing Australia's Great Barrier Reef, one of the world's most vital natural treasures—but they have not given a complete, easy-to-understand "big picture." What do tornadoes in Florida have to do with mud slides and thirty-foot waves in California, anyway? How do the many interrelated forces of ocean and atmosphere mix to bring such disparate effects to such widely separate regions? How do these effects come together to form a dynamic, global climate shift, and what is the full toll of these storms and droughts in terms of economy, ecology, and human life?

We'll try to piece together just such a big picture here. We'll also take a look at what scientists are doing—and have done over the years—to construct this picture and to continue filling what gaps remain with state-of-the-art science and white-knuckle observation. In a full view of El Niño, devastating weather and the human toll it exacts are threads that run throughout the story, as they will here. Hopefully, though, the perspective that emerges will be a fuller one than the headlines alone can provide. For El Niño is not only a fascinating and dramatic subject for study; the questions it poses and the answers it provides may be inextricably tied to the fate of the earth.

Climate research and long-range climate forecasting are both fields in which we are rapidly gaining fresh understandings. The earth and its weather is the laboratory of these scientists, and El Niño, by stirring up conditions in the lab, provides a great opportunity not only to learn more about El Niño, but also to learn more about the world's infinitely complex and constantly interacting weather patterns. More intimate knowledge of the vast systems that govern weather, and how they work in concert, leads us in turn to more accurate forecasts—as we have learned from the early prediction of the 1997–98 El Niño. These mid- to long-term forecasts can save lives and save economies by keeping people prepared for extreme conditions. Ultimately, though, and even at their most accurate, they only tell us what the weather will be; we remain powerless to change it, a fact that this past El Niño has driven home all too often.

Along with so many extraordinary developments in the sciences at the close of the millenium, we are moving into the age of the long-range forecast. We already have some ideas, hotly debated (if you will), about what the global climate trends are and to what degree they will continue and intensify in the next century. The forecast, unfortunately, is not all that good. We'll explore the degree to which El Niño is tied up in these trends and whether the increased incidence of El Niño, as the twentieth century draws to a close, is cause or effect (or neither) of these trends. The answers to the riddles posed by El Niño may, in the end, be key to understanding the fate of the planet and therefore of us all.

2

How It Works:
The Mechanics of El Niño

If you so much as opened a newspaper, read a magazine, or switched on a television in the fall and winter of 1997–98, chances are you heard about El Niño. The latest "mother of all El Niños" generated unprecedented media coverage due not only to its sensational effects throughout the United States and the world but because of our heightened awareness of the system, fostered in part by accurate predictions far in advance—the El Niño hype machine was already grinding to a start in the fall of 1997. But TV news footage and newspaper accounts of crumbling hillsides and neighborhoods smashed by twisters, dramatic as they may be, deliver only part of the El Niño story. When we see the destruction that results when

El Niño weather hits land we are witnessing only El
Niño's effects. These effects tell us that El Niño is
indeed a force to be reckoned with, but they don't
give us a very firm understanding of what El Niño
really *is*.

El Niño is in fact much more than a catchall
phrase for a laundry list of inclement weather around
the globe. Even the name El Niño obscures the whole
picture. When scientists refer to El Niño, they generally do so in the context of what they call ENSO—an
acronym that stands for the El Niño–Southern Oscillation. Even this daunting mix of Spanish and
techno-speak, which we'll get to in a little bit,
doesn't take everything into account: it leaves out La
Niña, a weather system that can be thought of as El
Niño's shier, somewhat chillier sister. And she's
sometimes know as El Viejo. Let's tackle this group
one at a time.

El Niño: The Pacific Coast in Hot Water

Of course, it's El Niño himself that gets top billing
and it's with him that we'll start. In its most basic
sense, El Niño is the name we've given to the phenomenon of higher than normal surface temperatures
during winter in the waters of the central and eastern
Pacific Ocean. "El Niño" has also become a shorthand
way of referring to the entire meteorological levia-
than of which these warm waters are but part. This

giant weather system referred to somewhat inexactly as El Niño is the subject of this book, and we'll try to be clear about exactly what we mean when we use the term here. The warm waters for which the name El Niño was originally coined is what we'll turn our attention to first, though.

These warmer than usual waters were first noticed and named, so tradition has it, by Peruvian fishermen plying coastal waters for the rich schools of anchovy (or anchoveta, as they're more properly termed) there; in the 1890s the name El Niño was officially adopted by science to describe the phenomenon. Because these warm currents, when they appeared, seemed to arrive in December with the onset of winter, the fishermen associated them with the Christian nativity and so named the effect El Niño—Spanish for little boy or, when capitalized as it is in this case, for the Christ child. So, put simply, when scientists tell us that we're experiencing an El Niño they mean that they have taken the temperature of the uppermost layer of water off the west coast of South America (and out to the central Pacific) at the equator and found it higher than normal. This span of abnormally warm water can stretch across the equator in a span the breadth of Europe in the largest cases, such as in the titanic El Niño of 1997–98. When we consider that scientists regard the Pacific Ocean as a bigger influence on climate than all the earth's rain forests put together, along with the axiom that warm patches of ocean water drive weather as do few other things on this planet, then it's easy to see why El Niño is seen as having as large an effect on climate as anything but the seasons.

When the Butterfly Beats Its Wings: Weather Connections and Teleconnections

Putting it simply in terms of hot water, however, does not remain a satisfying explanation for long; such simplicity raises more questions than it answers, because weather does not occur in a vacuum— every meteorological event, however small, inevitably causes a reaction in neighboring weather events, and those neighboring meteorological events correspondingly have an influence upon their neighbors. This is the complicated dance of interrelated weather systems that, with its subtle yet discernible rhythms, produces climate. The maxim "Climate is what you expect, weather is what you get" is no less true for having been so often repeated in discussion of El Niño. Understanding this saw is integral to grasping the essence of how El Niño works: not so much by generating weather on its own—because, as we'll see, El Niño is just as much a product of weather as it is a producer of it—but by altering the circumstances under which this weather takes place. Because of the closely interrelated nature of weather systems—and El Niño is an especially influential one—such displacement can have a domino effect with global repercussions. The repercussions? An increased likeli-hood of unusual weather throughout much of the world—the weather you get runs counter to what your region's climate would lead you to expect. You get inclement weather, and sometimes you get quite a lot of it.

It's hard to point to a single factor being responsi-ble for any incident of weather, or to any one episode of weather being responsible for the overriding dy-namic of a weather system. There's a famous political cartoon you may remember from your high school history text: illustrative of the way the Cabinet func-tionaries involved in the 1924 Teapot Dome scandal passed around the blame for the debacle, it depicts a circle of President Warren G. Harding's cronies pointing to one another in succession. As with the corrupt politicians in this famous political cartoon, looking to one factor as causing weather inevitably points to another. A corollary to this is that a weather event can simultaneously seem to cause and be caused by the same neighboring weather with which it is interacting.

There's an oft-repeated parable that is used to dis-cuss how small, singular, seemingly random happen-ings can have outsize influence on events even thousands of miles away: A butterfly emerges from its chrysalis in the South American rain forest. Perched on a tree branch, the butterfly flutters its wings gently to dry them. The tiny movements of the but-

terfly's wings create an infinitesimal disturbance in
the air around the creature, which in turn causes a
somewhat larger disturbance farther on—and so on,
resulting in a hurricane that batters the North American coast.

The parable of the butterfly is most often associated with what is known as chaos theory, a branch of
study in mathematics that strives to find the order in
seemingly random occurrences and natural forma-
tions. You may have seen chaos theory in action as the
underlying programming basis for fractals, those
multicolored, constantly undulating forms generated
by computers and often seen adorning computer
screen savers and T-shirts.

Chaos theory is itself often used to describe the
formation and interaction of individual weather
events and whole weather systems, which are inter-
connected series of weather events. In fact, the butterfly parable is used by chaos theorists to illustrate the
principle of sensitive dependence on initial conditions, a principle born from the mother board of a
computer being used for weather research. In 1961 a
meteorologist named Edward Lorenz was running
weather forecast models on one of the first supercomputers. One day Lorenz, wanting to review a particular forecast sequence, ran the data through the
computer again; to save time, he started at the middle of the sequence, rather than the beginning.

When Lorenz returned to the computer an hour

later, he found that the sequence had played out very differently from the previous time. When he backtracked, he eventually discovered that he had entered a piece of data to three decimal places—a measurement to the thousandth—which the computer had, in the first go-round with the data, initially read to six decimal places. The infinitesimal difference in the first number, so small as to exceed reasonable standards of scientific accuracy, not to mention the capability of the instruments at the time, translated into a great difference in the final set of figures. This lesson led Lorenz to believe that a totally accurate forecast was beyond the reach of science; it also laid the basis for computer models that have brought scientists closer to the goal of accurate forecasting than was previously possible. It also impressed even more deeply on them the degree to which something like a change of a few degrees in ocean temperature can yield vast changes from a great distance.

Now, the motion of a butterfly's wings may not actually be capable of stirring up vast storms whole continents away, but then again, it may. The parable of the butterfly underscores an essential point about weather in general and El Niño in particular: though individual weather incidents are easy to grasp in that they follow simple physical laws—actions beget reactions—their interactions with one another are so numerous and complex that identifying a single cause for the behavior of a weather system, or predicting how a large weather system will behave, can be very difficult indeed. Like the one that spawned chaos theory, some of the very first supercomputers—extremely powerful mainframe systems that dwarf familiar desktop models in size, speed, and memory capacity—were developed to compute the overwhelming number of variables that must be taken into account in order to correctly analyze and forecast the weather. Today's supercomputers are many times more powerful than their 1950s ancestors, but the complexities of how meteorological events interact with one another to form weather and weather systems challenge even their great power. And because every incident of weather has an effect on neighboring incidents, a butterfly's wings theoretically can stir up high winds across vast distances, through the chain reaction of neighboring weather incidents affecting each other down the line. Scientists call these long-distance interactions between weather events teleconnections, and they are integral to the huge weather system of which El Niño's warm waters are but a part.

ENSO It Goes: The El Niño–Southern Oscillation

We began with warm water off the South American coast because this effect has lent its name to El Niño. Now, though, let's enlarge our scope to look at ENSO—the El Niño–Southern Oscillation—encountered at the beginning of this section. The El Niño part of this term refers, as we have seen, to warm water conditions in the central and eastern Pacific Ocean; the Southern Oscillation is the seesaw between these warm water episodes and the cold water conditions which characterize La Niña. The Southern Oscillation also describes the seesawing of high- and low-pressure systems between Tahiti (which is in the eastern-central Pacific) and Darwin, Australia (which lies in the western Pacific). In El Niño years (when central and eastern Pacific surface temperatures are higher than usual), there are generally warm air and low pressure over Tahiti and generally cold air and high pressure over Australia. In La Niña years, when Pacific surface temperatures are colder than usual (and normal years, in which the Pacific is nonetheless cooler than in El Niño years), the pressure systems are reversed. As you may have suspected, the correlation of warm water in the central and eastern Pacific and warm air and low pressure over Tahiti and on east to the South American coast is more than a coincidence—it is, in fact, a key part of the ENSO machine.

In normal years, as we've noted, low pressure is found over Australia, along with the wet, warm weather that comes with it, while low pressure and dry, cooler conditions prevail in Tahiti and eastward on to South America. The normal, or neutral, conditions of low pressure over Australia and high pressure

over Tahiti are part of a Pacific-wide weather system
known as the Walker Circulation. The system is
named after Sir Gilbert Walker, a British oceanographer who first identified the east-west pressure seesaw
that comprises the atmospheric part of the circulation. Jacob Bjerknes, a hugely influential Danish
oceanographer, first described the workings of this
large-scale weather system and named the phenomenon in honor of the man whose work had laid the
foundations for his own. ENSO represents a disrup-
tion of the Walker Cycle. The best way to understand
ENSO, then, is to begin with an understanding of
how things look before ENSO throws a wrench in the
works.

A Very Large Bowl of Soup: The Walker Circulation

Since we started our discussion of ENSO with warm
Pacific waters, we'll start with cold Pacific waters for
the Walker Circulation—specifically, cold, deep water off the western coast of South America. When
normal conditions prevail, this cold, deep water continuously rises to the ocean's surface in a process
known as upwelling, bringing with it a host of nutrients that support all manner of marine life, from the
microscopic to the more complex forms such as, significantly, the anchovy. The cold, deep water wells up
to replace the warm surface layer. What has happened
to the warm surface layer? The answer is as simple as

it is hard to believe: it has been *pushed* westward by prevailing winds called trade winds. In non-ENSO years, there is actually about a half meter (a foot and a half) more water on the western side of the Pacific than there is on the eastern side!

You've no doubt been on the shore—any shore—on a blustery day and seen how a driving wind will impose its own will upon the water, flattening the waves and even creating crests of its own against their motion. On a still smaller scale you can witness this effect right now if you have a bowl of soup in front of you: when you blow with force on the side of the bowl nearest you, the topmost layer of chicken noodles is sloughed off the side being blown on—think of this side of the bowl as South America—and it piles up against the far side of the bowl—Asia's eastern coast. The trade winds—so named because they were the primary routes of maritime trade in the age of sail—perform this feat on an oceanic scale.

The trade winds blow north along the Peruvian and Ecuadorian coasts before veering west. Returning to our bowl of soup, if you blow hard right up against one side of the bowl—as the trade winds blow along the South American coast—some of the soup will move in the direction you are blowing. Most of it, though, will push out to the side, at a 90-degree angle to the path of your breath and toward the far side of the soup bowl. So moves our surface layer of warm water in an effect amplified by the unique dynamics of the ocean, pushed away from northerly trade winds at a 90-degree angle, to pile up on the far side of the bowl, or as it happens in this case, the Asian side of the Pacific basin.

So just as the eastern Pacific, stripped of its warm top layer, is continuously cooled by upwelling, the western Pacific, its warm surface replenished constantly with those waters torn from the east, maintains its warmth. A low-pressure system, as we have seen, is characterized by air that is warm and therefore lighter than cooler air. In light, warm air, evaporated water can rise high enough to form clouds of condensation that will eventually return to the earth and sea as rain, as happens in the western Pacific in normal years (and as is augmented in La Niña years). Where the cool, heavy air of a high-pressure system prevails, as it normally does in the eastern Pacific, water vapor is less likely to rise high enough in the atmosphere to form rain clouds. So, in the normal course of things, the Walker Circulation brings the monsoon season of heavy rains to Australia, Southeast Asia, and the Indian subcontinent. In Tahiti and along South America's Pacific coast, the drier climate for which the region is known holds sway, and upwelling of deep water keeps the waters nutrient-rich for the marine life upon which local economies depend.

The Walker Circulation represents the normal state of things, with the teleconnections between wa-

ter, winds, and atmospheric pressure systems perpet-
uating the cycle. The trade winds slough off the
warm water in the east, pushing it west; cold water
wells up to replace the lost surface water, cooling the
air above it and feeding a high-pressure system in the
east, which in turn keeps the trade winds on their
course. In the west, the extra warm water from the
east warms the air, fostering a low-pressure system
that in turn encourages the trade winds to blow in
that direction. In this low-pressure system, water
evaporated from the ocean and land is able to rise
high enough in the atmosphere to form rain clouds;
this process of condensation throws off energy, thus
warming the air and feeding the cycle, and so
on. . . .

What happens in ENSO years to throw the Walker
Circulation off course? We'll start with the trade
winds, bearing in mind that the process doesn't
necessarily "start" with them, because all parts of a
weather system are interdependent. ENSO, then,
"begins" when the trade winds slacken, thus blowing
less of the eastern Pacific's surface waters to the west.
With its top layer of warm water more or less intact
now, upwelling slows considerably in the eastern Pacific; this, combined with the warmth of the surface
water now left there, can cause the temperature of the
usually cool eastern Pacific—and by extension the air
above it—to rise substantially, creating a system of
low pressure.

Because of the huge volume of ocean involved, the warm water that "backslides" east when the trade winds weaken takes a while to get all the way to the South American coast, so water temperatures in the central Pacific are often the first to rise. This is why higher than normal temperatures in the central Pacific are frequently signs that an El Niño or ENSO may be on its way.

Meanwhile, in the west, the process is reversed. The ocean temperature cools as the surface layer diminishes, and the effect is augmented by an increased occurrence of upwelling. The air cools above the water, and a high-pressure system develops off the Asian coast and over Australia. The heavy rains and thunderstorms normally experienced in this region move east. The result is diminished rainfall, even drought, in Asia and Australia, and increased rainfall, even flooding, in South America. This is the condition we know as El Niño or, to be proper about it, the El Niño phase of the Southern Oscillation.

What about La Niña?

As we noted earlier, El Niño has a sister, La Niña (Spanish for "little girl"), so named by scientists to credit its opposite effects from the little boy. We tend to hear less about La Niña than we do about her warmer, more famous brother because her effect on the Western Hemisphere is less pronounced, or at least less immediately appreciable. Because the "Southern Oscillation" part of ENSO refers to the interaction between conditions that characterize El Niño and those typical of La Niña, calling the system the El Niño–Southern Oscillation means engaging in a bit of meteorological sexism. The El Niño, or warm, phase of the oscillation was the first to inspire research, what with its monsoonal failures and floods, so it has received billing where La Niña has not.

We, too, are less concerned here with La Niña than we are with El Niño, but we should give her her due because she is a part of ENSO (maybe someday, in a bow to equality, we'll know the system as ENLASO). In reality, it's not so much sexism as the less dramatic change in climate she brings about that keeps La Niña in obscurity. Whereas El Niño represents a reversal of the natural order, as described by the Walker Circulation, La Niña is merely a strengthening of conditions typical to Walker: stronger than usual trade winds helping to cause (and, in turn, caused *by,* as we need to keep in mind) even colder than normal surface temperatures in the eastern Pacific and even warmer than usual surface temperatures in the western Pacific. The result is, as with the Walker Circulation, a low-pressure system over Tahiti and South America's Pacific coast and a high-pressure system over Australia and Asia's Pacific coast.

La Niña's conditions can be thought of as Walker, but more so. How much more so depends on, as we have come to expect, many factors, but water temperature is a good indicator; the colder the waters off the South American coast, the greater potential severity of the La Niña. Hence La Niña is by no means benign, as it can visit disastrously heavy monsoonal rains upon India, Indonesia, and other parts of Asia while causing drought along the already arid South American coast.

SO—Is It Always El Niño or La Niña?

Now that we've established that La Niña is the cold end of the Southern Oscillation's seesaw (because of its cold South American coastal waters) and El Niño is the hot end, we see that the oscillation between high- and low-pressure systems in Darwin, Australia (in the western Pacific), and Tahiti (in the eastern Pacific) is also a seesawing between El Niño and La Niña. With this in mind, we may wonder if this means that we are always experiencing either El Niño or La Niña.

We've been defining El Niño and La Niña by the way in which they manifest sea-surface temperatures (SSTs, to scientists), which are either higher or lower than normal, and the way in which they encourage abnormal weather. But what do we mean when we speak of "normal" surface temperatures and "normal" conditions? In scientific terms, the word normal usually connotes a mean, or average; in this case a mean temperature or, more specifically, a mean surface temperature for a given part of the ocean for a specific time of year. These averages for different parts of the oceans in different seasons have been computed, using data compiled over the years by researchers, with much greater reliability in recent decades. Oceanographers, climate scientists, and others who rely on information about the ocean thus have a measure of what to expect for a given area in a given month of the year.

If the sea-surface temperatures in zones monitored by ENSO researchers spike to either .5 degrees centigrade above the norm or dip .5 degrees below it for a protracted period, an El Niño or La Niña, correspondingly, is under way. During periods when the sea-surface temperature stays more or less within this one-degree range, conditions are said to be neutral. Hence you have warm years, such as 1982–83, neutral years such as 1984–85, and cold years such as 1988–89.

If these deviations from the normal SST for a given section of ocean seem small, one needs to keep in mind just how narrow is the acceptable temperature range for life on the planet. As those who warn of the dangers of global warming often point out, a difference of only a degree or two in average annual temperatures can mean the difference, for example, between ice packs melting or remaining frozen, and therefore of more or less water being released into the global ecosystem, and on down the line through the many interdependent contingencies of weather. Or think about the effect even a small increase in our body temperatures has on the way we feel. The reactions that take place on earth do so within a range sufficiently narrow that variations of just a few degrees centigrade can be significant indeed. Especially when these temperature variations spread out over thousands of miles of ocean.

The 1982–83 El Niño, with sea-surface temperature deviations exceeding +3.5 degrees centigrade (6.3 degrees Fahrenheit), displayed what was at the time the strongest SST deviation on record. As in so many departments, however, the 1997–98 El Niño exceeded this earlier event in SST deviation from the norm: Pacific waters during this more recent El Niño were in some places more than 5 degrees centigrade (14 degrees Fahrenheit) above normal.

The SOI

Sea-surface temperature anomalies are but one important way for scientists to measure the incidence and severity of ENSO events. Another gauge is offered by the Southern Oscillation Index (SOI). This, as the name suggests, is a measure of the difference in atmospheric pressure between the two poles, or ends, of the seesaw of the Southern Oscillation—Tahiti and Darwin, Australia.

The Southern Oscillation Index is derived by subtracting the atmospheric pressure figure of Darwin, Australia, from that of Tahiti. (El Niño researchers have many more points in and along the Pacific where they monitor atmospheric pressure; readings from these two points, however, continue to figure most strongly in the calculation of the SOI.) When the Walker Circulation is in normal working order, the number that results from subtracting Darwin from Tahiti should be zero or close to it. This zero connotes the equilibrium between the two measurements found in neutral years. Under normal circumstances, the low-pressure system usually found over Darwin gives a negative reading (a typical number is −7 and the high-pressure system found over Tahiti is represented by a positive integer (in this case, +7 is more or less the norm).

When a cold (La Niña) or warm (El Niño) phase of the ENSO begins to take hold, however, this equilibrium is thrown off balance, either into the realm of the positive or negative. So, for instance, if Tahiti begins to experience lower pressure (say our initial figure of +7 drops to −7) and Darwin higher pressure (−7 increases to +7)—the hallmarks of the El Niño phase of ENSO—the reading will be a negative number (in this case, −7 − +7 = −14). With La Niña, the effect is simply reversed: Tahiti's positive number would rise while Darwin's would drop, yielding a positive number as the answer to the equation, Tahiti

– Darwin = SOI. Weak El Niños or La Niñas register an SOI reading of around 10, strong El Niños such as that of 1972, an SOI of 25 or less; and very strong El Niños such as those of 1982–83 or 1997–98 an SOI of 35 or more.

But How Does It Get Here? El Niño and North America

Now we know that ENSO is caused by an interacting system of air, wind, and sea that in turn causes rain cloud formation in the equatorial Pacific to shift east toward the South American coast. But what about *North* America? How is it that a weather system at the equator, even one thousands of miles across, wreaks havoc far north in the United States? The interdependence of meteorological forces is once again the key.

At a height of about 10 kilometers (5 to 7 miles), in the atmospheric layer known to scientists as the *troposphere*, winds circulate around the globe at speeds of up to 300 and at times exceeding 300 kilometers (about 190 miles) per hour. These winds, known collectively and individually as the jet stream, swirl their way poleward, blowing in a way consistent with the flow of water in the Northern or Southern Hemisphere. Maybe you're aware that water (or any liquid, for that matter) drains in a clockwise whirl north of the equator and counterclockwise south of the equator. The same is true of the jet stream—think of jet-stream winds as the individual streams of giant whirlpools of air draining at each pole.

Jet streams form where air masses of different temperatures come together. In the winter, when temperature contrasts are at their greatest, there are generally three temperature zones across the United States, Canada, and Mexico. These three climate zones in turn produce two jet streams at their borders, known as the polar jet stream and the subtropical jet stream. In non–El Niño years, the polar jet stream is normally stronger than the subtropical jet stream. The polar jet stream swoops down from western Canada, across the Northern Plains and Great Lakes States and into the Middle Atlantic States and New England. The subtropical jet stream, meanwhile, blows somewhat more placidly across Baja, California, and northern Mexico.

The jet streams are like rushing streams, influenced to go this way or that by the atmospheric "terrain." In El Niño years, the Pacific Ocean can push large "boulders" up in the streams' paths. El Niño's climate changes—generally, warmer subtropical temperatures—push these jet streams to the north. The polar jet stream moves up to central Canada, an area where temperature contrasts are not as great as along its usual path, and weakens considerably. With the polar jet no longer pouring arctic air down from Canada, the northeast United States experiences a milder winter. The subtropical jet stream, however, is strengthened in El Niño years. It moves in from the Pacific, hitting land in southern California and coursing across the U.S.–Mexican border until it cuts a swath across central Florida.

During an El Niño, as we have seen, the air above the Pacific Ocean is especially rich in moisture. Huge storms form far out at sea. The El Niño–strengthened subtropical jet carries these storms to the east and slams them into the California coast. The normally arid Southwest can receive dramatically higher rainfall levels. The Southeast also faces inundation. Finally, as we saw so dramatically in the 1997–98 El Niño, the deviant subtropical jet stream can visit tornadoes upon central Florida, an area that is not usually considered part of the tornado belt. The area hit by tornadoes that killed forty-two people on February 23, 1998, was, as Joseph T. Schaefer, director of the National Weather Service's Storm Prediction Center in Norman, Oklahoma, observed, "right under the jet stream."

The subtropical jet and the great size (and subsequent moisture raised by) the 1997–98 El Niño brought pronounced but typical effects to the United States: winter precipitation was a full nineteen inches higher than usual in San Francisco, a foot above normal in New Orleans, and an amazing twenty-one inches greater than usual in Tampa.

The jet stream also brought the United States and Canada a bit of the unexpected during the 1997–98

El Niño. On January 7, 1998, weather patterns altered by El Niño caused the subtropical jet stream to flare northward, shooting warm, moisture-filled air from the Gulf of Mexico right up into northern New York and Quebec. At practically the same time, the polar jet stream dipped south, dropping a cold, low-pressure system onto the same region like a bomb. The warmer, lighter air from the south sailed over the colder, heavier air from the north. The moisture held by the warm air fell as rain but when it hit earth—and roads and power lines and buildings—the much colder temperatures there froze it immediately. The result was one of the most severe ice storms in the region's history, replete with flooding and loss of life, as more than two inches of rain fell on some parts in a matter of hours.

But How Does It End?

With all the ways in which El Niño's forces—wind, water, temperature, and pressure—interact with and exacerbate one another, it may seem as if an El Niño, once under way, should just continue to grow stronger and stronger. The ocean's equilibrium, however, is maintained by an internal pendulum: giant undersea waves.

These waves, termed Kelvin waves and Rossby waves by scientists, are closer kin to tidal waves than to the waves one generally sees at the beach. We've

already seen how an El Niño begins with the slackening of trade winds that usually push surface water
from the eastern Pacific to the west. The warm water
"piled up" in the west sloshes back east, warming
that part of the Pacific and retarding upwelling,
which causes further warming. Well, to say the water
"sloshes" back east is a rather inelegant way to put it,
in the eyes of an oceanographer or one who studies
fluid mechanics. A more refined way of describing the
action of the eastward-bound warm water is to say
that it moves in the form of a Kelvin wave, propagat-
ing from the western Pacific toward the South American coast. Kelvin waves, which can be many
kilometers long, move slowly (though not as slowly
as Rossby waves, as we shall see) through the ocean.
They can exist only within 5 degrees latitude of the
equator, so they are uniquely suited to their task of
serving up El Niño.

While Kelvin waves herald El Niño's birth,
Rossby waves sound its death knell. A fully developed El Niño event begins to send Rossby waves out
toward Asia. These waves pass through the ocean so
slowly that their movement is barely perceptible. Nor
do they create an impression on the surface, as does a
tidal wave or the waves you see on the beach. They
are, however, huge—hundreds or thousands of kilometers long and a couple hundred meters deep. Below the ocean surface, the first one hundred meters or
so of a Rossby wave slide in one direction while the

bottom one hundred meters or so slide in the other. After months or even years, this sliding, tumbling motion can take a Rossby wave to the Asian end of the Pacific basin, whence it then reflects back. The water a Rossby wave carries with it can alter interior ocean temperatures so as to "cancel out" the El Niño effects originally set in motion by a Kelvin wave.

As a reflected Rossby wave passes through the central and eastern Pacific, El Niño's high sea-surface temperatures begin to cool and the Pacific's temperature becomes more uniform. In the 1997–98 El Niño, we began to see manifestations of this process in May and June; SSTs began to drop rather dramatically during his period.

It's worth noting that, in addition to providing El Niños with their beginning and end, the roles played by Kelvin and Rossby waves are key to the Pacific Ocean's status as sole home to El Niño. These waves do exist in the planet's other great ocean, the Atlantic, but the Atlantic's considerably smaller basin means that its warming periods are much shorter lived than in the Pacific. Even the slow-moving Rossby waves produced by such a dynamic bounce too quickly off of the American and African coasts, from which they are reflected back. Once reflected, as we have seen, these waves bring ocean temperature back into equilibrium in the areas through which they pass.

We've come to see that behind El Niño's dramatic

and often deadly effects lies a story of varied and interdependent natural forces at work—at times on an almost unbelievable scale. Such are the minute and massive forces that shape weather on this planet. For years, though, ENSO events were known only by their effects; it took many years of careful study and analysis by researchers in a variety of disciplines for El Niño's behind-the-scenes story to emerge. ENSO's effects caught the attention of early climate scientists and—almost as important—the governments that funded their research, in the form of monsoon failure in Asia, India, and Australia and as manifest in floods in the Americas. As individual threads of the ENSO tapestry were unraveled, technological innovations and fortuitously timed El Niño events came together to provide scientists with both the tools and the "laboratory" (i.e., the Pacific Ocean and the climate zones affected by El Niño) conditions with which to construct the picture of El Niño we have seen in this chapter. Now, with this picture in mind, let's take a look back to see how scientists arrived at this construction.

3
El Niño's Long History

When news reports forecasting this last El Niño began rolling in during the fall of 1997, many of us weren't sure if we had encountered this sort of thing before. The words *El Niño* may have had a faintly familiar ring to those who remembered the devastation of the 1982–83 El Niño, but the sporadic nature of media reporting on the phenomenon—concentrating mostly on its effects, and only while they were in progress—led to long stretches when El Niño was all but invisible to the general public. As a result, a lot of people were left wondering, "Wait, is this El Niño something new?" or "This is the weather thing that began in 1982, right?"

The truth is, neither of these speculations is the

case: El Niño has been with us for aeons, literally
thousands of years. Our first record of the effect dates
back some five hundred years, and serious scientific
inquiry into its causes and effects began over a century ago.

Earliest Accounts

The earliest written accounts we have of El Niño's
effects come to us from the Spanish conquistadors
who invaded South America in the 1500s. These ra-
pacious Spaniards halted their wholesale plunder of
the South American continent for sufficient time to
note the warm current off the Peruvian coast, but
made no connection between it and the periodic rains
that would bring rare water to the Peruvian coastal
desert, one of the driest coastal regions on earth.
These rains, then regarded as occurring every seven
years, are generally believed to have aided the con-
quistador Pizarro in his ruthless conquest of the Incan
empire. Certain scientists, who have gained an idea of
what weather was like in the distant past by learning
to read clues from such sources as tree rings, speculate
that there was an El Niño at the outset of Pizarro's
conquests that provided water and food for his horses
in a region where neither would ordinarily have been
available.

Witnesses to the Past: Searching for El Niño's Clues

Looking at the rings of certain species of trees is but one of several methods scientists have at their disposal as they try to ascertain the weather and climate of the distant past. The scientific detectives who search for these clues are known as paleoclimatologists, from the Greek *paleo,* which means "ancient," *climate,* which we already know about, and *-ology,* which literally means "writing" but has also come to mean "the study of." So a paleoclimatologist is someone who studies—and hence often writes about—ancient climates.

Reliable, complete records of such data as temperature and atmospheric pressure go back only some 150 years, and while weather and climate are certainly referred to in even the oldest of historical sources, these accounts are necessarily subjective. They are often valuable in giving a paleoclimatologist a historical reference point to test against physical evidence such as tree rings. But often these scientists are looking back to a time so distant that it predates written history and indeed humankind's very presence on the earth.

When scientists cannot use scientific records or historical accounts for information about the weather and climate of the past, or when they wish to corroborate what they have learned from a subjective source with more objective data, they turn to what they call proxy data. This is information derived from such sources as trees and other silent witnesses to the earth's climatic history. Some of the other places paleoclimatologists look for clues to ancient climate are in deep, very old ice packs found at the earth's poles and on mountaintops, and in the sediment left behind from ancient floods and found on the seafloor, in coral, and in fossils of plant pollen.

These natural witnesses to ancient climatic history may be silent, but paleoclimatologists are skilled detectives who know how to get them to "talk" and divulge their clues about the past. Scientists who are looking specifically for the clues left behind by ancient El Niños use a variety of the proxy data generally available to paleoclimatologists, which can include flood sediment, tree rings, coral, and ice cores, and fossil pollen found in some unlikely places.

Those scientists engaged in ice-core sampling, for example, extract deep, cylindrical cores of ice from a polar ice cap, such as that which can be found over the large (though not actually so large as it appears in Mercator map projections) island of Greenland and the Antarctic continent, or from mountain glaciers at high elevations. They then analyze these cores in a laboratory, utilizing a number of techniques such as carbon-14 dating, which can determine the age of any organic material in the sample, and gas spectrography, which provides a breakdown of the ice's chemical composition. Some of these core samples are drilled down to the underlying bedrock, often at depths exceeding a kilometer. It is important that the sample be from a mass of ice that has experienced very little or no melting and refreezing over the course of its formation—this condition provides clear separation between each year's layer of snowfall and ice buildup.

Ice-core sampling has turned up evidence of an El Niño that possibly occurred circa 2200 B.C. Dr. Lonnie Thompson, a professor of geological science at the University of Ohio and one of the preeminent researchers in this field today, has drilled core samples through several kilometers of glacial ice, in some cases reaching bedrock in such sites as the aforementioned Greenland and Antarctica. His research has increased our understanding of, among other things, global warming trends.

In 1993 Dr. Thompson led a team of researchers up a remote Andean peak to collect core samples from a glacier near the summit. When he analyzed the ice he found evidence of a massive drought that occurred circa 2200 B.C. Such a finding was consistent with the effects of El Niño in the region, leading to speculation that a large ENSO event was indeed the cause. This is about as far back as inferential evidence of El Niño through scientific observation goes.

Just as clues to the climate of the past can accumulate in layers of glacial ice, so too can clues build up in the layers of silt left behind by flood events. And just as the most useful ice-core samples for researchers come from ice packs that have undergone minimal melting and refreezing, flood deposits from regions where flooding is rare yield the most fruitful analyses. Finally, just as with ice-core samples, carbon-14 dating techniques can be performed on layers of flood sediment to approximately date specific layers and to establish a chronology for successive layers.

Gary Huckleberry, a geoarchaeologist at Washington State University, is in the midst of researching flood deposits in Peru's coastal desert, which is not only one of the driest coastal regions on earth but an ideal spot to look for evidence of El Niño. Huckleberry is conducting his research at a site called Quebrada de Los Chinos, which lies in the Moche River valley in the northern part of Peru, near Trujillo, Peru's second largest city. Farmers long ago diverted the Moche River at high elevations to irrigate their crops, causing the river's lower tributaries to become dry canyons for the most part. These dry canyons are especially useful to Huckleberry in finding evidence of past El Niños because it is almost exclusively El Niño that causes the rare flooding of these dry riverbeds.

Huckleberry concentrates his study on a twelve-foot-high bank of sand from one of these dry riverbeds, known locally as *quebredas*. The bank contains regular thin layers of organic material, which can be analyzed through carbon-14 dating. His preliminary research has turned up evidence of eleven different El Niño–related floods dating back over 2,500 years. In addition to providing some of the earliest evidence of El Niño in South America, Huckleberry's research is a boon to archaeologists studying the region's "rich history of complex societies," as Huckleberry puts it.

Huckleberry's research can work in hand in hand with that conducted by, for example, Dr. Steve Bourget from the University of East Anglia, whose recent excavation in Peru of an Incan burial pit has unearthed evidence that has led him to conclude that the human skeletons he has found are those of people offered as sacrifice to appease an angry sea god during a particularly strong El Niño occurring around 1500. (This, you will recall, is an era in which we've seen evidence of a number of strong ENSO events).

The study of tree rings, known to scientists as dendrochronology, is, as we have seen from the earlier example of Pizarro, very useful to paleoclimatologists. You may recognize in dendrochronology the word *chronology,* which means "to construct a written record of time's passage." That is what paleoclimatologists hope to do when they study tree rings; it is also what the tree rings do on their own, in their own language, that these scientists have learned to decipher.

You probably know that you can find out the age of a tree by counting the rings in its trunk—one ring for each year the tree has been alive. What you may not be aware of, however, is that these rings vary in size depending on the weather conditions in the year a given ring was formed. Years in which conditions are favorable for a tree's growth—generally those in which rain is plentiful—leave their mark inside a tree as thicker rings, whereas arid years tend to produce thinner rings. The reason for this is elementary: each ring is essentially the girth the tree added to its trunk that year, the dark delineation of which is the mark left by the old bark layer.

Because species of trees that are sensitive to climate variations leave a record of these changes, dendrochronology has proved invaluable to researchers searching either for initial evidence of past El Niños or for corroboration of sources such as written historical accounts. Some of the leading dendrochronological research is conducted at Columbia University's Lamont-Doherty Earth Laboratory, which is also one of the preeminent centers for climate and, by extension, El Niño.

Dendrochronologists at Lamont-Doherty have found evidence of an El Niño that occurred in 1000 A.D. This ENSO left its mark in an especially robust growth ring for this year in samples from trees in northern Arizona, which is consistent with El Niño–influenced weather patterns. Lamont-Doherty's findings from Arizona correspond with those from samples recovered from trees in Santiago, Chile, another area that is typically under ENSO's rain clouds.

Coral-core sampling is similar in principle to research on both tree rings, because it involves analyses of a life form, or at least its skeleton, and ice cores, because it involves drilling and the extraction of a historical record embedded in vertical layers put down over the ages.

Dr. Julia Cole, of the University of Colorado at Boulder, conducts X-ray analysis of coral reefs in the Galápagos Islands. Coral, being very sensitive to even minute variations in ocean temperature, is particularly affected by the hot water of El Niño, as we have seen with the damage that has been visited upon Australia's Great Barrier Reef during this El Niño. This susceptibility to ENSO-induced warm waters, though unfortunate for coral (and ultimately all of us, because of the integral role coral reefs play in the global ecosystem), makes coral samples excellent sources of proxy data pointing to past El Niños.

Dr. Cole's research has not only turned up evidence of El Niños dating back hundreds of years but has led to the discovery that, three hundred years ago, ENSO events were half as frequent as they are today. It is not known why this is; the answer, when it comes, may contribute to our understanding of worldwide climate trends over time, including global warming.

It is to tree rings and sediment—in this case, from lake beds—that we turn again for evidence of what scientists believe was among the first, in 1835, large El Niños to significantly affect the new American nation. In this instance, the available tree ring and sedimentary data corroborate what are, from that time, sketchy meteorological records that strongly suggest that an ENSO event was under way in that year. The year 1835 represents the beginning of the history of El Niño in the United States, though this was not yet known. Native Americans living on the West Coast were no doubt at least aware of El Niño's effects, if not of the full scope of the phenomenon itself; the European-derived settlers just beginning to take permanent root in the area before the gold fever of '49 were not. One of the most serious early impediments to creating a lasting settlement at the site that would later become Los Angeles was a hurricane that slammed into the coastal outpost that year—the only hurricane in Los Angeles's recorded history.

The Christening of El Niño

From later in the nineteenth century come the first references to the warming of the sea just after Christmas as "El Niño." As we've already seen, tradition—which we've no reason to doubt in this case—has it that Peruvian fishermen named it thusly because of the coincidence of its periodic arrival with the nativity of the Christ child. Far from being a savior to these fishermen, however, the marine El Niño imperiled their livelihood by sending schools of fish away—usually to the north, where the Colombian fishing industry would often become the beneficiary. It would not be until the end of the century, however, that serious scientific inquiry into El Niño would begin. And when it started, it was not because of El Niño's warm waters off the South American coast, but because of a drought thousands of miles away, in what was then the jewel of the British imperial crown—the subcontinent of India.

Monsoon Failure and the Search for Connections

India is a country that is arid much of the year; its immense population and supporting agriculture depend mightily upon the summer rains. This dramatically increased rainfall generally hits eastern India in June and covers the entire country by mid-July; its arrival heralds the advent of the summer monsoon season. India's summer monsoon is actually only one of the country's two seasonal rain periods but it is of much greater significance to India's well-being—and, in India's days as a British colony, the imperial weal— than the winter monsoon. The summer monsoon can deliver up to 80 percent of the annual rainfall upon which India depends. The failure of this monsoon can spell a year of misery for the subcontinent.

Eighteen-ninety nine was just such a year. Deprived of its major season of rainfall, India suffered greatly. The punishing drought brought widespread crop failure, leaving untold thousands to die of starvation. Thousands more fell prey to the epidemics of cholera and plague that followed. This was an echo of what had happened in India in 1877, another year that the monsoon had failed and, though it was not recognized at the time, the last ENSO event before that of 1899. That earlier experience had set British meteorologists scrambling for clues that might give them advance warning of the next monsoon failure. While one avenue of research, which sought connections between drought years and sunspot activity, did not ultimately prove promising, other directions taken by this general investigation made some of the first scientific headway toward understanding the global interconnectedness of weather patterns—the teleconnections we saw in chapter 2.

It was noted, for example, that drought in India often corresponded to the same condition in Australia. In India, Henry Blanford, who was essentially the chief meteorologist for the Indian colonial government, reported in 1881 that he believed that the springtime snowfalls on the Himalayas and upon the Eurasian landmass were related inversely to the success of the Indian monsoon. This avenue was thought promising—as, indeed, it still is regarded today—but it did not lead at the time to a reliable formula that could be used to predict the failure of the monsoon.

Walker and the Southern Oscillation

The acuity of the suffering that came in the monsoon's absence, combined with India's prominence in
the British empire, kept improved understanding of
monsoon failure a scientific priority. Useful connections were not found or fully confirmed, however,
until Sir Gilbert Walker, the head of the Indian Meteorological Service in the time following the 1899
drought, made the key association that lies at the
atmospheric heart of ENSO.

Walker had believed for some time that weather
systems at a far remove from one another could nonetheless exert a mutual influence. Searching for these
teleconnections—though they were not yet known by
this name—was something of a fashion among the
Victorian scientific community. Walker sought not
only to gain some practical insight into the forces
behind the failure of the monsoon but to begin to
prove that some of these teleconnections existed. He
searched for them in records of atmospheric pressure
and temperature, which had by then been collected
reliably for more than sixty years; in sea-temperature
readings; and in records of snow and rainfall from as
many locations as he could get his hands on.

Walker's examination of data from a wide variety
of sources, as recorded by a similarly diverse range of
recording stations, built in many ways upon important research performed just before the turn of the

century by the Swedish meteorologist H. H. Hildebrandsson. Hildebrandsson had amassed a decade's
worth of atmospheric data from sixty-eight reporting
stations scattered about the globe and had in his findings traced the first outlines of the Southern Oscillation. Hildebrandsson, in addition to noting certain
general relationships between the trends in data from
locations at a far remove from one another, discovered
an apparent "seesaw" in pressure between South
America and the region of Indonesia and Australia.
Hildebrandsson believed that this large meteorological effect was caused in some way by forces that were
polar in origin. As Walker came to believe many
years later, Hildebrandsson thought the answer
might be found in examination of snowfall data.
Walker, in studying the monsoon, duplicated
Hildebrandsson's search with a greater number of reporting stations recording for him an even greater
abundance and variety of data.

Walker was also aided in his search for connections
by the monsoon failure of 1914, also an El Niño year.
Just as the massive El Niño of 1982–83 came to
provide meteorologists with a real-life, real-time laboratory in which to test their assumptions about
ENSO, thus greatly advancing our understanding of
the phenomenon (which enabled us to predict the
1997–98 El Niño months in advance), this drought
observed by Walker as it unfolded helped him begin
to unlock the pieces of the ENSO puzzle.

We must once again bear in mind that this search for correlations with the failure of the Indian monsoon took place without knowledge of El Niño's warm surface waters off the South American coast. Walker's research lay in atmospheric pressure readings. Looking at these readings for locations in Australia, the equatorial central Pacific, and Chile, a number of seemingly linked anomalies caught his attention. In 1924, after he had retired his post, Walker conclusively identified what he called the Southern Oscillation, the pendulum swing of atmospheric pressure as read between these sites. (Today, you'll recall, readings for determining the strength of the atmospheric pressure swing in the Southern Oscillation are taken at Darwin, Australia, and the island of Tahiti.)

Walker constructed the first Southern Oscillation Index (SOI), intending that it give warning of a coming monsoon failure and serve as a gauge in measuring the severity of the atmospheric forces behind such a failure. Walker's formula was a Rube Goldberg–like agglomeration of pressure, temperature, and rainfall data, onto which he had grafted factors such as lake levels, river flood stages, mountain snowpack depths, and even sunspot activity. Years later the formula for determining the SOI was pared down to essentially the atmospheric data, which was the only set found to have a direct and determinable correlation between

measurements taken in the South American regions
versus those from the Indonesian and Australian area.

In discovering that the high-pressure system that
brought drought to India was tied to an anomalous
low-pressure, rain-encouraging system in the central
and eastern Pacific, Walker not only made the first
steps toward giving India advance warning of monsoon failure but uncovered the first solid evidence of a
teleconnection. His research, however, lay fallow for
some time after his death in 1959.

El Niño's Great Dane—Jacob Bjerknes

It was not until the mid-1960s that other scientists
began to build substantially on Walker's foundation.
Again, it was a significant El Niño event that provided both the impetus and much of the data that led
to a surge in our understanding of the phenomenon.

The 1957–58 El Niño was not only a strong one
with an adverse impact on a number of economies,
notably the guano industry in Peru; it also unfolded
against the backdrop of the much-heralded International Geophysical Year. This coincidence garnered
the system—not yet understood as an integrated
whole of ocean temperature and atmospheric pressure
swings—an unprecedented degree of concentrated international scientific attention.

An effort was made by the scientific community to
record as much information as possible on the

changes undergone by key atmospheric and oceano-graphic indicators while the El Niño unfolded. This data, as it turned out, proved to be invaluable in uncovering a complete picture of the air-sea interactions at work across the Pacific Ocean.

Among the foremost investigators into El Niño's climatic mysteries at that time was a Danish oceanographer at the University of California, Jacob Bjerknes. Bjerknes analyzed all the available data from the 1957–58 El Niño and had by 1966 reached the conclusion that El Niño's warm waters were brought about by a slackening of northwest trade winds, which caused a rise in sea level in the eastern Pacific, which in turn reduced the rate of the upwelling of deeper, colder ocean water.

By 1969 Bjerknes had developed a climatic model that spanned the Pacific, integrating prevailing winds, large ocean waves, water temperature, up-welling processes, and huge tropical storm systems into a whole of global weather interdependencies. He named this climate model the Walker Circulation, to honor the pioneering work performed by Sir Gilbert Walker in discovering the Southern Oscillation. Most important, Walker had predicted that the governing dynamic in the Southern Oscillation would be found in the interaction between the Pacific Ocean and the air that lies above it. And it is Bjerknes's Walker Circulation, you will remember from earlier in the book, that the forces comprising El Niño disrupt.

ENSO: Looking for the Big Picture

With the beginnings of a complete working model of
the Southern Oscillation—in the form of the Walker
Circulation—in hand, climate scientists approached
El Niño from a wide variety of research angles in an
effort to further unravel its mysteries. Many scientists, of course, continued to collect oceanographic
and atmospheric data while others investigated such
avenues as paleoclimatology, as we have seen here, in
order to begin to understand the frequency and severity of past El Niños.

As ever, those scientists who have gathered and
analyzed climatological data from the past, and as
weather unfolds, have had as their goal not only a
more nuanced understanding of the processes that set
El Niño and the whole of the Southern Oscillation
into motion but also the improved ability to predict
the El Niño and La Niña phases of the Oscillation
that this refined knowledge of ENSO's mechanics
would engender.

In these twin aims, scientists have been greatly
aided by two of the signal developments of the late
twentieth century—computers and space flight. Con-
versely, some of the earliest achievements in both
these fields were spurred by goals of improved
weather prediction. We have already seen how the
need to crunch the daunting number of variables involved in creating models of weather so as to forecast

its changes gave rise to the first supercomputers, and how this interaction inspired chaos theory. Similarly, some of the first craft sent into orbit in the early days of the space program were weather satellites. For the first time, humans were able to gain a vantage point from which to view even the largest weather systems as they undulated across the globe. Finally being able to see "the big picture" aided scientists greatly in visualizing the far-flung interactions of atmospheric systems with one another. Once again, however, El Niño's dramatic appearances acted as spurs to move research forward.

El Niño Back in the Spotlight

The 1972–73 El Niño, the strongest El Niño in almost a hundred years, provided such a major spur, in the form of concentrated international attention on the phenomenon's effect on natural resources. This was an El Niño that unfolded during a year of anomalous weather around the world. Massive drought in Africa and Asia, exacerbated by El Niño, caused widespread famine and generated serious concerns among the world community about the security of food supplies. El Niño became one meteorological plague among the many visited upon the earth that year.

For the nation of Peru, however, the 1972–73 El Niño was a disaster that overshadowed all the other unusual weather of that year. Its anchovy fisheries, already depleted since the collapse of the guano industry earlier in this century, failed dramatically due to the decreased upwelling of deep-water nutrients, a hallmark of El Niño's warm surface waters. (Guano, which was for years Peru's major export for a variety of agricultural and industrial applications, is the hardened excrement of certain species of seabirds; these birds fed on the anchovy, which for a long time led to their protection from large-scale commercial fishing.)

The collapse of Peru's fisheries wreaked havoc on its fragile economy and struck repercussions throughout the world's food supply as farmers scrambled to replace the feed and fertilizer functions of the anchoveta with crops grown on land that would have otherwise gone toward feeding humans. The experience led Peru to conduct scientific inquiry it had long deferred into the warm waters off its coast. Until this point, scientific study of ENSO had tended to focus on the atmospheric part of the seesaw and then, generally, as it affected the western end of the picture— Australia, India, and the Indonesian islands. With the prod of the 1972–73 event, and with fresh sets of data in hand from that El Niño, the Peruvian government lent its support to Peruvian scientists who joined a worldwide scientific effort to further unravel El Niño's mysteries with, again, the goal of more accurate and earlier prediction of the onset of an El

Niño event and the particular meteorological effects that a given El Niño might favor. The weather-generating capabilities of large patches of warm ocean water, though consistently far-reaching in their effects, do not always follow the same pattern—no two El Niños unfold in exactly the same way, nor do they always encourage the same type of weather in a given region. Knowing in advance that an El Niño is on its way could help direct agricultural and economic strategies in such a way as to minimize losses in production, allow for an increased readiness to respond to such eastern El Niño–related disasters as flooding, and ultimately save many lives in both the long and short terms; if one could also know how an approaching El Niño might manifest itself, all the better.

Curiouser Still: The Odd El Niño of 1976–77

El Niño's unpredictable nature was driven home to researchers by the next event, that of 1976–77. That year's El Niño was a strong one that, in its effects, contradicted the composite picture of El Niño that scientists had theretofore constructed using data from the events of various years. Instead of drenching the western United States with rain and contributing to a milder than usual winter in the Northeast, the 1976–77 El Niño brought record cold and snowfall to eastern North America and drought to the West—in California, it was the worst in history. In arctic Canada the cold was such that polar bears did not go into hibernation. In a reversal of the 1972–73 event, which despite all its catastrophic effects saved Americans tens of millions on their heating bills with an unusually warm winter, the 1976–77 El Niño saw up to 85 percent of the nation covered with snow at one time. El Niño research remained a priority as expressed in the funding it received from the world's governments and it was with some confidence that climatologists assimilated data from this most recent El Niño, anomalous though it was. The scientific focus on El Niño following the 1972–73 event proved to be enduring, marking that El Niño as the first great watershed in our understanding of the phenomenon in the space and computer age.

Caught by Surprise: The 1982–83 Episode

It was with this sense of being close to coming to terms with a working predictive model of El Niño that a number of the world's leading climate scientists convened in November 1982 at several conferences in the United States and abroad. Among the presentation of papers on a number of topics, an explicit consensus emerged among the conferees: there would be no El Niño that year. This view was not a surprising one, given that it echoed the thrust of several papers presented to general agreement at a number of conferences in previous weeks and months and even the direct pronouncements of Peru's senior science officer. The assertion was not a blind one, based as it was on observation of factors thought to be key early-warning signs of developing El Niños—easterly winds at the equator and early warm waters off the Peruvian coast that were thought to always foreshadow a full-blown warming of the coastal and central Pacific; this was known as the onset phase: the easterlies were thought to characterize El Niño's buildup phase. Scientists monitoring these activities found no strengthening of equatorial easterlies nor any unusually warm water off the western South American coast; absent these developments, thought to be necessarily symptomatic, they concluded that the world would be spared that year.

Thousands of miles away, however, in the central Pacific, quite a different story was unfolding, told by the sea in water warming to an alarming 5 degrees centigrade higher than normal for the given location at that time of year. While the climatologists were pronouncing the year safe from El Niño, a very large El Niño was indeed heating up but not where they had trained themselves to look. What those convened at Princeton did not know was that the largest El Niño to date was just beginning.

That most climatologists missed the brewing storm, so to speak, is not altogether a surprise, despite the intensive work that had been conducted on ENSO since the woes of 1972. The El Niño that was under way in late 1982 was anomalous in the ways that we have already seen and, indeed, in the fact that its earliest manifestations began as late as November. And, quite literally, the scientists' view was clouded: the Mexican volcano El Chichon had erupted earlier that year, throwing tons of dust into the atmosphere, which hampered the photographic and thermographic capabilities of satellites observing the Pacific. The proximity of El Chichon's eruption to this El Niño gave rise for a time to a school of thought that regarded volcanic events, including deep-sea volcanic venting, as possible triggers of El Niño. This view seemed to receive a degree of validation in 1991, when the eruption of Mount Pinatubo in the Philippines preceded the El Niño of 1991–92, but a statistical analysis of the frequencies of both events later deemed the correlation meaningless.

The way El Niño caught them by surprise in 1982 brought home to scientists the limits of their statistical modeling of El Niño. Once one ventures earlier than the mid-1950s, ocean-temperature records are spotty and those that exist are often unreliable. So the sea-temperature data for the computer-forecast models that the climatologists were devising had come from a very limited number of El Niños (most of which have been covered here, beginning more or less with the El Niño of 1958–59 from which Bjerknes gathered most of his data). With the anomalous effects of the 1976–77 El Niño a fresh memory and the

1982 El Niño catching them back on their heels, scientists were having it made very clear to them that El Niño events could vary wildly in their onset and the course they took thereafter. A more reliable forecasting model of the ENSO warm phase would require a larger and more varied pool of El Niño data.

Planning a TOGA Party: A Big Science Response

For oceanographers and meteorologists, improving the quality of their oceanographic data was an issue that at that time was very much on the front burner. The scientific community addressed this challenge with a very ambitious plan for a decade of concentrated study. The plan was to place an enormous array of sensor-equipped buoys across the Pacific Ocean, where they would work in concert with data-gathering and communications satellites, surface vessels, and planes to provide a wealth of data, much of it in real time, on the ocean and atmosphere. The TOGA (Tropical Ocean and Global Atmosphere) project, often cast simply as a reaction to scientists being caught off guard by El Niño in 1982 (and that El Niño's subsequent ferocity), was in fact in its earliest planning stages when El Niño took all but a very few forecast models and their creators by surprise. The spirit of anticipation surrounding the TOGA program was such that it may even have contributed to scientists being caught off guard by the 1982–83

El Niño—when looking to the future one sometimes loses full sight of the present.

It did not take scientists long, however, to realize that they had a nearly full-blown and rapidly intensifying El Niño on their hands in mid-November. Ever aware that observation of El Niños in progress—the real-time goal of the TOGA project—provided the best hope for figuring out El Niño's full dynamics, scientists scrambled to glean what precious data they could from this El Niño. They borrowed and applied what principles they could from the incipient TOGA project, all the while lamenting that the buoy-satellite array was not in place to record this of all El Niños. Because as scientists watched and recorded and theorized as best they could, all hell was breaking loose around the world.

Havoc in its Wake: The Toll of 1982–83

The 1982–83 El Niño was, until the 1997–98 event, the strongest of the century and possibly the strongest since the beginning of recorded history. Worldwide, it caused an estimated eight to thirteen billion dollars' worth of damage and killed more than two thousand people and countless livestock and wild animals as it scorched half of the world with drought and drenched the other half with flooding of near biblical proportions. It impressed scientists with record-setting readings and anomalies that bordered on the bizarre. It left, quite simply, a stunned world in its wake, its food supply threatened once again in echoes of the 1972–73 event, and it became the instant benchmark for El Niño. It also provided a wealth of information to scientists who overcame their initial surprise to muster a truly heroic data-gathering effort, so its advent came to represent a watershed in our understanding of the phenomenon. For all these reasons, it is worth taking a further look at it here.

In the Americas, the 1982–83 El Niño brought a historic season of coastal flooding. The west coast of the United States, California in particular, was battered by a parade of rainstorms and the huge waves these storms stirred up as they swept in from the Pacific. The rains combined with snowmelt from the warmest winter in United States history to cause mud slides up and down the coast and all along the Colorado River. The waves, which at times exceeded thirty feet, shattered waterfronts all along the California coast. The various forces of nature (which even included a couple of storm-generated tornadoes near and within Los Angeles) that the 1982–83 El Niño unleashed upon the western United States destroyed houses, businesses, roads, and crops to the tune of more than one billion dollars' worth of damage, not to mention the scores who died and hundreds who were left homeless.

In northern Peru the story was similar. El Niño's

ground zero was devastated by the heaviest rainfall in recorded history. Areas where the *annual* rainfall was typically six inches were inundated with eleven feet of rain over a span of a few weeks, and some rivers carried one thousand times their usual flow. The reduction of upwelling integral to El Niño's warm waters predictably decimated Peru's fisheries. In Ecuador also, relentless rains caused misery through flooding and mud slides, killing some six hundred people and causing again more than one billion dollars in damage to crops and property. Farther north, though, in Central America, El Niño was exacting its price in drought. Scorched crops fell short of their average yields, and withered grazing lands provided scant sustenance to starving cattle that eventually had to be destroyed in the thousands.

Way out in the Pacific, Hawaii, typically afflicted by drought in El Niño years, was slammed by a rare hurricane. The French Polynesian Islands were pummeled by no fewer than six cyclones which left twenty-five thousand homeless in Tahiti.

On the other side of the Southern Oscillation, searing, punishing drought was the rule. The Asian monsoon, so prominent in early research on the Southern Oscillation, failed mightily during this El Niño. Australia experienced what was by far its worst drought of the century, turning almost the entire southern half of the continent into a sere wasteland in which huge dust storms—one, which struck Melbourne in February 1983, covered an area exceeding seventy-five thousand square miles—could kick up in a matter of minutes, as they did frequently in a season of unusually high winds. The gusts also spread huge brushfires, fed by drought-parched vegetation, with such deadly speed that they claimed seventy-five lives and left eight thousand homeless.

Australia's wildlife, especially its cattle population, were even less fortunate: withered grazing land and woeful cattle prices combined with the inescapable facts of deadly heat and insufficient water conspired to seal their fate as more than 100,000 head were either killed by the elements or destroyed. Not surprisingly, farm income in Australia fell off by half in El Niño's wake, with losses totaling several billion dollars. And with livestock herds requiring more time to rebuild than crops, it took several years for the country's agriculture to get back on its feet. Creatures of the bush, such as kangaroos and emus, suffered from the same conditions as did their ranch and farm counterparts, with many of the same deadly results—the final stroke coming not from a rancher's rifle but from the often slower, crueler hand of nature. Perhaps of greatest consequence to the ecological well-being of the planet was the large-scale bleaching and death of coral in Australia's Great Barrier Reef, a vast and extremely temperature-sensitive ecosystem that can be thought of as a rain forest of the deep.

El Niño left its mark in a trail of misery across the Pacific and in Asia and finally on the Indian subcontinent and in Africa as the monsoon successively failed to arrive in each region. In the Philippines and Indonesia, drought decimated harvests and famine felled more than three hundred persons. In monetary terms, the damage reached almost one billion dollars. India's situation provided a bleak echo, with crops destroyed and shortages of fresh water prompting fears of outbreaks of jaundice and other diseases.

Southern Africa, already on the edge of famine after two previous years of subpar rainfall, was pushed over that precipice by the 1982–83 drought. Particularly hard hit were the tribal "homelands" within South Africa, where the very direct reckoning of wealth in terms of cattle made lost herds all the more poignant a blow. Crops suffered shortfalls reaching 70 percent, bringing additional malnutrition and disease to a part of the world that had already known more than its share. Also imperiled throughout the region were endangered species who foraged with desperation for food and water throughout the veld. In Botswana's Chobe National Park, wild elephants, rendered tame by a titanic thirst, sought water at human camps.

In addition to all the destruction it brought, the 1982–83 event produced some scientific marvels that impressed even the most experienced of climatologists. Not only were the data astounding—record-breaking drought and deluge became the routine around the world for this El Niño; individual effects also gave scientists pause. The westerly trade winds off the South American coast did not only slacken, which as we have seen is both characteristic of and integral to the El Niño process, but they actually reversed, piling even more warm water than is usual for El Niño onto already high sea levels in the eastern Pacific.

El Niño's huge tongue of warm water licked thousands of miles into the central Pacific and northward where it joined an initially unrelated patch of warm water off of the California coast. California fishermen, engaged in a fruitless search for crucial catches of indigenous fish populations, instead encountered rare tropical species and common tropical game fish such as marlin. The 1982–83 El Niño produced a pool of warm water in the Pacific of such size and intense warmth that twelve years later an eight-inch-high wave of water heated by that El Niño survived in a five-mile-an-hour trek across the Pacific. Perhaps the most impressive scientific observation to come out of the 1982–83 event was recorded by scientists at Atmospheric and Environmental Research, Inc. (a private research concern) in Cambridge, Massachusetts: they found that El Niño's effect on jet-stream circulation and upon the trade winds had affected the angular momentum of the earth through space in such a way as to actually lengthen our days by a fraction of a second at the phenomenon's height.

This El Niño also came to take the blame for all manner of ills that arose after the effect itself had dissipated: In the eastern United States El Niño's warm, wet spring bred far more mosquitoes than usual, which led to encephalitis outbreaks; the same conditions proved favorable to rodents in New Mexico, leading to rare outbreaks of bubonic plague there; in Montana hot, dry weather drove rodents to lower elevations in search of food, and rattlesnakes followed, leading to a marked increase in snakebites throughout the state in the summer of 1983; on the west coast, seafloors resculpted by El Niño's storms tricked surfers, leading to a host of spinal injuries; and in Oregon, where warmer than usual waters had brought sharks to places where they were not usually found, a sudden rash of attacks on humans by these misplaced beasts followed.

It would be difficult to overstate El Niño 1982–83's impact on the research landscape. The episode's severity, and the surprise it gave to a scientific community seemingly on the cusp of fully understanding the phenomenon, not only caught but held the attention of people around the world. There was a good deal of El Niño hype but when the actual event proved its equal, El Niño took hold of the public consciousness in an unprecedented way. The attention El Niño received on this go-around translated into a renewed commitment to El Niño research around the world. The funding landscape for ocean and climate research became quite a bit more fertile and the "big science" commitment to projects like TOGA assumed a public sense of urgency concomitant to that within the scientific community. This sentiment not only sustained the ten-year study but aided it in spawning the groundbreaking TAO (Tropical Atmosphere and Ocean) array. TAO proved itself invaluable in predicting and tracking the 1997–98 El Niño, as we shall see.

With the 1997–98 El Niño now in the books (so to speak) after having been observed in real time and thrilling detail by the TAO array, the 1982–83 event will inevitably come to represent a transitional period in El Niño study. It was the "El Niño of the Century" before the 1997–98 installment blew the crown from its head—the most recent very strong warm water ENSO event and therefore the one from which scientists have the best data. In the era before TOGA and TAO, the 1982–83 El Niño was instrumental in shaping scientists' theoretical models of how an El Niño unfolds.

A Floating Hubble: TOGA and TAO Begin a New Age

The year 1985 did not contain an El Niño but it ushered in a new era of climate and ocean study nonetheless. The year marked the beginning of the TOGA program's intensive, El Niño–inspired examination of the Pacific and the air above it. From this time until the study closed in 1995, TOGA made great strides toward understanding the big picture and nuances of ENSO.

An unusual El Niño did, in fact, occur during TOGA's run, giving scientists a chance to stalk their quarry directly, so to speak. The El Niño which began in 1990, though strong at its peak, did not yield the dramatic effects of the 1982–83 event. It did, however, last for five years, its warm water not dissipating until 1995. This was by far the longest El Niño in 130 years of reliable record-keeping, which in some researchers' minds, begs a question: Was the "length" of this extended warm water episode merely a reflection of TOGA's refined data-gathering techniques? Even if this was the case, however, it would still necessitate an accommodation of this new facet of the ever-surprising phenomenon.

TOGA scientists in fact had El Niños to study during almost the entire run of the study. The 1990–95 marathon was preceded by an El Niño that ran from 1986 to 1988. As planned, TOGA proved invaluable in compiling a reliable and complete record of these El Niños as they unfolded. When scientists speak of TOGA, however, they tend to focus on its legacy. In particular, the program provided a wealth of dependable data to be used as fodder for computer simulations. These simulations in turn proved capable of providing seasonal-to-interannual prediction of the sort of rise in Pacific surface temperatures that would herald the onset of El Niño. This work represented a tremendously satisfying validation for scientists engaged in attempts at climate prediction, a field long held at the fringe by many other scientists.

TOGA's most valuable legacy, however, is the TAO (Tropical Atmosphere Ocean) array. We'll take a closer look at TAO and its various components in chapter 9 but it is all but impossible not to at least touch on it in any historical discussion of El Niño. El Niño researchers enthuse about TAO in much the same tones of reverence as astronomers reserve for the Hubble Space Telescope. The comparison is an apt one because TAO, like Hubble, has engendered a leap in the quality and quantity of data retrieval within its field. Like Hubble, this leap has brought about a corresponding jump in understanding of the subject under study: TAO has enabled scientists to see how an El Niño develops and runs its course in minute detail.

The TAO array, at its most basic, consists of seventy buoys that span a full third of the earth's circumference. These buoys are linked to satellites for constant, real-time monitoring of ocean and atmosphere. The data gleaned from these sources is simultaneously fed into number-crunching supercomputers to obtain computer-forecast models capable of continuously readjusting themselves in response to changing conditions in real time.

TAO began its life as the buoy-satellite component of the TOGA program. The TAO array as we know it today became fully operational in 1994. When TOGA ended in 1995 this element of the program, linked to climate-modeling computers as described earlier, lived on. The array was barely operational in time to add its data to the TOGA monitoring of the very long 1990–95 episode, but those who studied El Niño knew it was only a matter of time before they had the TAO array fully at their disposal and ready to record and analyze an El Niño from its earliest inception through to its decline. Not only would they be able to trace many atmospheric and oceanographic facets of the next El Niño every step of the way, their computers would be modeling constant scenarios as to what would happen next.

Of course, TAO was not only of use in studying El Niño, so the scientists involved with this project weren't exactly sitting around on their hands waiting for the next event. TAO's real-time monitoring of air and sea conditions provides a trove of data under any prevailing conditions. Nonetheless, the further study of El Niño had provided the initial impetus for TOGA and TAO, so it was with some excitement that researchers began to receive forecast models from the array's computers suggesting that a major El Niño was on its way.

The climate scientists and oceanographers at NOAA (the National Oceanographic and Atmospheric Administration, a government agency that plays a major hand in administering and servicing TAO along with a global consortium) did not of course wish El Niño's wrath upon anyone, but they could scarce believe their good fortune in having an El Niño—particularly one that promised to be a very strong event indeed—approach so soon after the array was operational. What became increasingly hard to believe in fact, even for the researchers themselves, were the forecast models they were getting, which kept pointing to a stronger and stronger event.

The big question before the onset phase of this El Niño—the initial warming of water in either the central or eastern Pacific—was whether this event would live up to its advance billing. For not only were the TAO-based predictions dire in and of themselves but they were greatly amplified by the media. Prudent, science-based caution soon gave way to hype that, when unfulfilled in the event's earliest months (especially in California), caused a certain lapse in public vigilance. By December and January, however, scientists monitoring the TAO observations and forecasts knew that El Niño was not only under way but that it was huge. Indeed it was only a matter of time before the large swath of very warm water scientists were seeing in the Pacific began to manifest itself in storms that battered the western United States.

As January became February, El Niño 1997–98 bared the teeth that, thanks to TAO, scientists monitoring the phenomenon had been able to see all along. At all times, even before El Niño's effects became discernible, we were able to keep tabs on the spreading pool of warm water that fuels the system. Even more impressive was the performance of the models based on TAO: scientists knew a full year in advance that an El Niño was on its way—and it took hold and developed just as the models had predicted.

As we have by now been amply informed, the El Niño of 1997–98 turned out to be "the mother of all El Niños," eclipsing even the mammoth 1982–83 event by just about any measure. Because it was the first El Niño to unfold under the watchful eye of the TAO array, because it proved the efficacy of long-range computer forecasting in a very public way, and most of all because of the unprecedented force it unleashed, the 1997–98 El Niño is one that will figure prominently in future histories of the phenomenon.

4

California in the Crosshairs

Like Godzilla, the 1997–98 El Niño hulked its way onto the California landscape with ease and a vengeance. When the initial forecasts came out in June 1997, Californians began to brace for what was predicted to be the worst El Niño in some years. In 1982–83, El Niño struck California with both devastating drought and torrential rain, rendering California once again helpless before the weather monster. Since the initial impacts of El Niño are caused by huge convection clouds that linger high above the Pacific Ocean, while jet-stream westerlies push these clouds toward the California shores, the Golden State in essence becomes the barometer for El Niño. Remember the myths about California falling into the ocean? After witnessing the devastation from mud slides, flood, and wind damage, it almost makes the average person want to pack his/her bags and move to Nevada. "We've thought about moving," one local resident said, "but this is what California is all about." If earthquakes don't make the residents "tremble" then what's a little rain here and there? Really, though, much of the damage that stands to hurt the California landscape is still lingering deep within the grounds: mud slides.

Think of the California landscape as a sponge. This simple analogy serves to illustrate how the land absorbs heavy amounts of rain over and over until it is saturated and can simply absorb no more. "When the rain would come it came like buckets. Literally sheets of rain. Then it would be clear for a couple of days; then here we go again," one resident of suburban Claremont exclaimed. All across the countryside, roads were washed out and houses lifted from their foundations only to serve as fodder for nightly news broadcasts across the country. Literally speaking, mountains were on the move.

The 1982–83 El Nino caused one hundred million dollars' worth of damage in California. High winds, big waves, and torrential rains triggered mud slides throughout the area that killed several and left many more residents homeless. Winter storms enhanced by El Niño also accounted for the destruction of highways and recreational facilities along the coastline.

Drivers traveling along the famous Pacific Coast Highway were inundated with sludge and mud from San Diego to San Francisco.

Seemingly chaotic in nature, these mud slides were no surprise to anyone familiar with El Niños from the past. During the 1982–83 El Niño, mud slides caused millions of dollars of damage to the California landscape. When the bill for the 1997–98 episode is finally tallied, it seems likely that 1982–83's damage records will fall alongside all the meteorological marks this past El Nino has toppled.

In February 1998 President Bill Clinton issued emergency relief funds to California to help alleviate damages exceeding a half billion dollars. "We're very well aware of all the difficulties you've had. . . . We're doing everything we can do to help," proclaimed Clinton in granting thirty-five of fifty-eight California counties disaster-relief funds. Governor Pete Wilson declared forty-two separate states of emergency. The Federal Emergency Management Agency (FEMA) allocated funds totaling over 10 million dollars to storm-battered victims, and another 4.8 million dollars in low-interest loans were approved by the U.S. Small Business Administration to help small businesses cover damage inflicted by the storms. Seven thousand citizens qualified for these loans to help alleviate costs not covered by insurance or for those whose homes are unlivable due to disaster.

Falling Hillsides and Rivers of Mud

Heavy precipitation not only brings the possibility of
leaving towns under water and bankrupt, but it also
increases the chance of a landslide. Debris flow and
mud slides are perhaps the most unpredictable and
chaotic of geological occurrences. Often increased
precipitation in the form of snow covers the mountainous regions of California making the skiing
community extremely happy, while folks living on
beachfront views of the Pacific in Malibu check to see
if their luggage is still in the attic. Heavy snowpack,
for instance, may be perfect at the time for skiers and
snow lovers alike but when the spring currents flow,
the water melts and makes its way into fissures and
cracks down to the bedrock beneath, gradually loos-
ening the earth below and eventually receding due to
the weight of gravity. In fact the threat of a landslide
remains long after the actual rains have fallen, seemingly playing craps with chips of bedrock. "The
lucky residents at best will only hear about the catastrophes on the news. The content are residents who
live across the street and watch as their neighbor's
house falls below. And the unlucky are those whose
house falls. The truly unfortunate souls are the ones
without insurance," Clara Petit, a Pacifica resident,
said. "One morning I woke up and I could see across
the hillside. I said to myself, 'The house is gone?' It's
something you dream about." Unfortunately, to in-

sure a home that resides on a cliffside costs a substantial amount, and often homeowners end up rolling the dice.

The possibility of a landslide can loom for months even years after storm systems desist. The bedrock that lies several hundred feet below the surface absorbs rain making it more malleable and likely to crumble. These geologic processes are at work at all times, even into the late summer. Even when there is drought, landslides are still likely. Recurring rain systems, though, will act as a catalyst for eventual widespread destruction. In the early eighties a slide three thousand feet long, two thousand feet wide, and two hundred feet deep formed in Malibu several months after the rain had ended. It happened during the height of the dry season.

The most immediate danger from the persistent heavy rains of El Niño is that of debris flow and mud slides. Mud slides are generally larger than debris flow. As heavy rains saturate the soil, the earth becomes so moist that it literally slips off the bedrock. Mud slides usually occur on shallow slopes, while debris flows run down from steep inclines. Debris flows are created when heavy precipitation causes the top layers of soil to essentially become a stream of dirt, rocks, and trees. During the most recent El Niño, safety nets were set up along Route 101 in Pacifica in order to catch loose debris. "Driving along Route 101 is scary sometimes," one resident said.

"You travel down the road and you see these big nets.
. . . After you drive by you start thinking that any
part of the mountain can fall right on me. . . . I
think a lot of people are scared." The Bay area was
inundated with relatively small debris flows, causing
millions of dollars of damage. Officials in California
predict that slides could cause up to one billion dollars in damage.

The ravaging mud slides and debris flows of El
Niño 1997–98 claimed lives as well as homes. Thousands of brave cows trudged helplessly to their deaths
trying to free themselves from the sludge. San Ber-
nardino and Chino cows tried to resist mud patches
leveling off at three feet. In total almost seven thousand cattle were overcome by falling debris and mud
slides. Meanwhile two California highway patrolmen
were tragically swept to their death when their car
literally dropped into the Cuyama River near Santa
Maria. An Orange County man was killed in a mud
slide that took him by surprise in February; residents
nearby described their encounter with the sliding
mud as like "being trapped in a washing machine."
People swept under by mud slides in Orange County
described one perilous situation: "I was just rocking
and rolling and desperately crawling my way to the
top of wherever I was. . . . Every second, you're trying to keep your hands in front of your face to create
a pocket so that you can breathe. . . ." Nine people

died during late February storms that bombarded the already waterlogged California countryside.

Sinkholes also plagued the California roadside during the 1997–98 El Niño. Interstate 15 became crater central after the moist soil underneath gave way creating holes larger than three football fields. A seventy-mile stretch of Highway 1 was damaged, leaving residents on edge. In Tijuana eight hundred residents had to flee their homes and move to safe havens in order to avoid a massive catastrophe. Sewage systems also began to falter as the increased water pressure caused many systems to break altogether. Sewer water left areas in San Diego spoiled while some rivers like the Santa Margarita absorbed excess flow. Sixteen million gallons of raw sewage spilled into the sea near the Los Angeles–Ventura county line. A one-hundred-yard stretch of Highway 166 was eroded by an over-flowing Cuyama River, causing major delays and millions of dollars of damage. Of the feelings prompted by Mother Nature's force, one resident said succinctly, "It makes you seem so small."

Even money is no match for El Nino's fury. Unfortunately, new homes only a year old became victims of the 1997–98 episode. Houses priced at around 1.5 million dollars hung over cliffs awaiting their turn to drop off the frontier and into the Pacific. In San Diego County million-dollar homes vanished while others teetered ever closer to the edge of disaster. So much rain, it seems, caused negligence on the part of homeowners as well, many of whom forgot to check their gutters, thereby causing them to snap and collapse under the harsh precipitation conditions. Even if the house didn't fall into the ocean it could have been badly damaged when rain started pouring into the basement.

In early February 1998, the rain fell hard on southern California. Areas across the state were drenched by almost two inches of rain per hour. Some travelers were overwhelmed when floodwaters rose to the hoods of their cars forcing many to swim for their lives. The Pacific Coast Highway was shut down because of scattered debris, while winds of almost seventy miles per hour ravaged the countryside, knocking down trees and telephone poles and damaging houses. Flash-flood warnings were declared across most of southern California. Flooding prompted several closings of highways, government buildings, and even some airports. Santa Barbara's airport was closed for several hours while crews furiously tried to impede floodwaters. Road crews working day and night declared war on sinkholes and craters that ruined roads and highways. The Oakland Public Works Agency was filling about 150 holes a day. Crews in San Francisco, too, were filling potholes at an extraordinary rate. Workers repaired holes at 157 locations during a seven-day stretch in mid-February. Close to 140 million dollars was spent on road repairs by the beginning of March.

High Drama and Humanity

The extensive damage occurring during February 1998 could have provided sufficient material for a book by John Steinbeck. By mid-February precipitation levels rose to almost record-breaking levels. Each week the national news headlines spelled out impending doom for the California countryside. "Will it ever end?" and "Here we go again," were trivial catch phrases for Brokaw, Rather, and their like. Everyone from New Britain, Connecticut; to Pasadena, California; from Duluth to New Orleans had El Niño on the mind. In California, however, this Hollywood script was real—that is to say, there were deaths, property loss, dreams swept off mountainsides, and especially the loss of little things such as photo albums and family heirlooms. But the more one looks at California and other states torn apart by nature's fury, the more a humane picture emerges. When the going got tough the tough got going. Literally thousands of volunteers made themselves available to aid and assist people who needed shelter from the storm.

The National Guard with their CH-47 Chinooks helped to evacuate victims caught by rising waters or aided in bringing food and medical supplies to people stranded. Furthermore, in mid-February, when a landslide ruptured a Shell Oil pipeline, dozens of volunteers and workers braved harsh conditions to bring the spill under control. Volunteer workers also helped in sandbagging efforts and mud-slide relief situations. Catastrophe brought out the best in Californians.

Down in the Flood: A Season of Record Rains

Much of the damage from the 1997–98 El Niño was attached to the furious rains that pelted the Golden State. For instance, work crews, roofers specifically, endured losses as a result of having to wait around for the rains to desist. Sometimes levees would break spilling thousands of pounds of water onto incomplete work sites. One company constructing a new helicopter field was overcome by floods. Half of the newly constructed airfield was under water. In Escondido, a Valley Center High School project experienced delays from flooding, costing thousands of excess dollars. In many cases workers are left trying to clean up excess water flow before the actual work can be done, and this type of situation costs thousands of extra dollars, which the company itself usually has to cover. It creates a catch-22; how can you fix the leaks in the roof when it won't stop raining?

During February 1998, California received an onslaught of rainfall spurring not only hurricane-like conditions but tornadoes as well. Each successive storm prompted a faster more immediate response. Crews trying to stave off floods endured long hours mitigating damage while also trying to sandbag against rains just over the horizon. San Diego crews were thrown into a state of emergency weeks before the storm systems arrived. In August 1997, scientists warned state officials of the impending El Niño, which could easily and swiftly damage coastal shores in excess of 100 million dollars. During the 1982–83 El Niño much of the California citizenry was unprepared. Storms leveled houses and beachfront businesses, they demolished roads and drenched basements. As a result thirty-three oceanfront homes were left destroyed while over three thousand other homes received extensive damage. Another thirty-five million dollars was spent to repair recreational facilities.

Predictions of precipitation rates at three times the normal put many farmers on edge, too. California's agricultural infrastructure was hit hard by El Niño conditions. California's multimillion-dollar lettuce crops fell short of expectations. Farmers in Arizona made good, though, by planting more lettuce crops than usual in anticipation of California's shortages. Shortages mean higher prices for consumers and higher profits for the farmers planting the cash crop. Other Californians faced the impending doom of floods to their crops. Avocado growers, however, were excited about the bad weather. Increased rain levels alleviated water prices and helped to nurture avocado and citrus crops. Cut-flower businesses felt the heat, though. Heavy winds were responsible for damaging thousands of dollars' worth of flowers. Furthermore, bad weather and poor road conditions made it hard for consumers to stop in. On Valentine's Day heavy rains detoured many flower buyers, sending most of them to the local drugstore for the standard box of chocolates. Strangely, though, for some lovers the heavy rains were probably the perfect backdrop for a candlelight dinner.

Tornadoes as well as flooding caused damage to California's landscape. In late February 1998 twisters touched down during fierce storms in Huntington Beach, ripping apart storage sheds and trailer parks. Fortunately no one was injured and the twisters were mild, nothing compared to the ones that hit Florida or South Dakota later in the year. Nearly simultaneously, another twister hit Long Beach ripping up trees and street signs but remaining relatively harmless.

Imagine mud slides, tornadoes, heavy winds, and flash flooding all occurring at the same time. The California landscape, in essence, became a punching bag for the brunt of the El Niño–driven storms. With reckless abandon these storms hit almost without warning. Dark, monstrous clouds lurked their way over the Pacific loaded with thousands and thousands of tons of rain ready to saturate the lands below. As one resident put it, "I looked over the hill one day and saw nothing but black clouds, it was like Godzilla was stumbling toward us, only unrecognizable because of all the dust he was kicking up along the way."

Surfers and Fishermen: El Niño's Beneficiaries in California

El Niño is a boon for some sea lovers, though. During the 1997–98 episode, surfers enjoyed gigantic waves while almost record-breaking tides pushed their way up to the already damaged California coast. One storm spurred swells as high as twenty feet, helping to create walls of waves as high as forty feet. Companies were even holding contests, offering thousands of dollars to the surfer who could ride the largest wave. "It teaches you a new appreciation for the ocean. Shows you how bad Mother Nature is. Even at night you lay back and listen to the tide rush, each wave crashing. It's beautiful, man!" one surfer exclaimed. Because of the warm water, as much as ten degrees warmer than usual, surfers in Oregon were able to surf without the normal bodyguard of a wet suit. "It's like taking a bath."

Skiers in Lake Tahoe, too, benefited from the excessive precipitation brought by the 1997–98 El Niño. Each week during the winter, snowpack levels continually grew. Fresh powder was spewed from the atmosphere creating perfect back-bowl rides along the edges of mountainsides. Folklore, as it is in the nineties, rests primarily on stories from El Niño's past. In 1982–83, storms helped to generate almost eight hundred inches of snow. Skiers and snow lovers love to reminisce about the record-breaking snow-falls from that year. In the 1997–98 El Niño, legend became reality once again. Ski resorts flourished with each new storm system, receiving ten inches, fifteen, sometimes two feet of new fresh powder. Ironically the same storms battering the oceanfront laid down perfect skiing conditions for vacationers across the West.

Likewise, fishermen benefited from unusual fishing conditions on the outer banks of the California shoreline. Because of the warm water swells lingering off the coastline, fish usually found much farther south were seen off the coast of the San Francisco Bay area. Mako sharks normally found in warm waters were spotted in Monterey Bay as early as September 1997. Marlin were spotted as far north as Oregon, pleasing fishermen and fish lovers alike in the Pacific Northwest. In Santa Monica Bay large schools of barracudas, yellowtail and bluefin tuna were spotted, pleasing sushi lovers in California.

El Niño's Crawling, Flying, Biting Aftermath

During an El Niño, ecological anomalies such as these occur not only offshore, but onshore as well. Biblical plagues of grasshoppers and locusts swarmed parts of the California countryside. In April 1998, a courthouse in Indo, California, was "flooded" with grasshoppers, forcing jurors to seek insect-free grounds outside. Supermarket parking lots in parts of Anaheim were "repaved" with these winged insects. Grasshoppers usually seek rural countrysides as their havens. Because of the unusual weather, specifically the excess rainfall, the numbers proliferated throughout 1998, causing millions of insects to migrate into more urban settings. The hoppers were everywhere: shopping plazas, schools, even museums.

Mosquitoes and butterfly populations were also affected by El Niño 1997–98. Although it's hard to gauge population levels, mosquitoes historically tend to thrive on such lush precipitation conditions. Along with their pestering bites, mosquitoes tend to be accompanied by diseases such as malaria or dengue fever. Butterfly populations, too, are hard to read, but some species may benefit from El Niño conditions while other species may be temporarily wiped out because of landslides or floods. With the abundance of rain, however, desert flowers hosted thousands of butterfly eggs, consequently bolstering the populations of some species such as the Painted Lady.

Unfortunately, the high winds of the 1997–98 El Niño stirred trouble for California's elephant seal community. The string of rainstorms that hit California in mid-February were directly to blame for the deaths of almost three hundred seals. High winds pushed tides to come crashing in against the rocks, pummeling the seals as they tried to catch fish off-

shore. "The ecological ramifications brought on by an
El Niño of this size are immense, sometimes devastating to local animal populations," one resident said.

As might be expected, El Niño 1997–98 caused
the tourism industry in California to suffer as well.
Downpours, mud slides, and hurricane-like activities
detoured thousands of tourists from visiting the
Golden State. Travelers were not willing to take the
risk of planning a vacation with the possibility of bad
weather looming. As a result, in some areas business
was down 25 to 50 percent. The West Coast is a safe
haven for vacationers from the East and Southeast,
who come to relax and soak up some rays. The onslaught of storms prompted thousands of visitors to
seek out other places, however, such as the Caribbean
and Florida.

Coming to Terms with El Niño and the Future

Gauging public sentiment on El Niño is somewhat
more difficult. There are no figures highlighting the
emotional strain brought on by losing one's house, no
charts to diagram the apocalyptic feeling this weather
phenomenon has conjured. "It's on everyone's mind,"
one resident said of the 1997–98 El Niño. "You can't
go out and have a normal conversation anymore; literally everyone has El Niño on the mind." Whether
Californians are just in awe of nature's fury is up for
debate. In today's world of high technology that

yields fast-moving computers and high-powered weather satellites it seems paradoxical—considering that the initial use of the computer was for weather forecasting—that people still linger in coffeehouses and in their neighbors' backyards pondering the weather. If this is any indication of where technology stands next to Mother Nature then we might reconsider our definition of high-tech. Throughout the course of California's history, nature has provided beauty but played a rather ominous role: earthquakes, dust bowls, massive flooding, and now El Niño. Yet only with today's sophisticated technology are we finally realizing that some of these catastrophes may have been linked to El Niño all along. Scientists are now only at the beginning of what will be years of research and investigation. With careful analysis of the most recent El Niño, scientists will begin to understand the hows and whys of this very complicated web.

It seems that Californians will not soon forget El Niño 1997–98. The destruction that has occurred and that has yet to be reckoned will certainly be a burden on California's economy. How much money will it actually cost to rebuild roads and homes, clean beaches and waterfronts when it's finally over? And, Californians ask themselves, does it ever end? Experience has taught scientists to expect El Niño's return in three to seven years. Over the last twenty-five years El Niño has inexplicably occurred more frequently than normal, prompting many to believe global warming is to blame. Will it be in California's best interest to construct more durable structures? If we know El Niño will recur indefinitely shouldn't states start preparing for the distant future? These are some of the questions our elected officials might try to come to terms with in the wake of the "El Niño of the Century."

5

Different Stops Along the Jet Stream: El Niño in the United States

In the last chapter we saw just how devastating El Niño can be to California. Looking at meteorological charts, it is not difficult to see why: The El Niño–strengthened subtropical jet stream passes right over southern California. As we saw in chapter 2, this jet stream carries with it huge storms formed in the moisture-rich Pacific and slams them right into the California coast. We also learned that, in El Niño years, both the subpolar and subtropical jet streams are pushed north. The subpolar jet moves up to the Canadian border and the subtropical jet alters the usual course it cuts across Mexico to flow just north of the U.S.–Mexico border. We can follow the story of the weather El Niño brings to the United States along these altered jet streams.

The West Coast is, of course, where the jet stream and the El Niño–inspired storms it carries from the Pacific first make landfall. It usually bears the brunt of El Niño's effects. El Niño manifests itself in a steady parade of storms that batter the coast and wreak the kind of devastation in California that we read about in the last chapter. Washington and Oregon can also receive significantly more precipitation during an El Niño, as they did during the 1997–98 episode, but this is not considered typical.

The storms of the "typical" (we must remember that no two El Niños are identical in their effects) El Niño make their way across the South along the subtropical jet. The Southwest and West Texas generally experience above-average precipitation and below-average temperatures while an El Niño is in effect. In the North, however, the Mountain and Plains States tend to record somewhat lower precipitation levels than usual; winters in the Pacific Northwest, which are generally very wet, tend to be drier than normal during El Niño.

In East Texas and in the Southeast, storms forming in the Gulf of Mexico tend to combine with moisture delivered by the jet stream to create extremely wet conditions in El Niño years. The rainfall suffered by these areas can be every bit as intense as that experienced by the most vulnerable spots along the California coast. El Niño can also bring an earlier tornado season to these places, and the shift El Niño inspires in the jet stream can transform places usually safe from tornadoes into disaster areas. This, as we have seen, is precisely what happened with such tragic results in Kissimmee, Florida, in February 1998.

To the Northeast, meanwhile, El Niño generally brings unseasonably mild winter temperatures but also a somewhat higher total rainfall than is usual. The Midwest shares these mild temperatures but tends to receive less than normal precipitation during El Niño years.

The Pineapple Express and the Western United States

If we consider the portfolio of weather that comprises the typical El Niño's effects upon the United States we see that the extremely powerful 1997–98 El Niño manifested itself in a way that was very true to type. The 1997–98 episode did manage to distinguish itself with a few surprising twists in the prescribed El Niño plot, but its effects were, on the whole, consistent with what scientists have come to expect from El Niño in the United States, if more intense than usual.

This, indeed, was very close to how meteorologists predicted the 1997–98 El Niño would play out. Predictions for the "El Niño of the Century" were largely on the mark for North America. Granted, some predictions did not pan out—ice storms, for instance, did not come to pass in the Southeast—but trends such as a mild winter in the Northeast, anomalous rainfall in desert areas such as Las Vegas, and a suppressed Atlantic hurricane season were forecast with impressive accuracy.

One essential dynamic scientists could not successfully forecast, however, was that of the jet stream. The jet streams that cross North America do not only shift to the north during El Niño; they also tend to flow more erratically. One often-seen effect during El Niño is the forking of the subpolar jet into two streams. When this happens, the southern fork tends to be the stronger of the two. It is familiarly termed the pineapple express for the way it quickly shunts huge storm systems from the mid-Pacific to drench California's northern coastal regions with rain that usually would fall on Oregon and Washington.

Meteorologists anticipated that the pineapple express would be a key player in the 1997–98 El Niño. Their prediction that it would begin shuttling storms to California early in the winter inspired forecasts of triple the normal rainfall for California. The fork did not occur for some time, however, leaving all El Niño's excess moisture in the north. Rather than experience the foreseen El Niño effect of less than normal precipitation, Washington and Oregon received more than triple their average rainfall and snowfall for the month of January. Meanwhile Californians derided El Niño as "El No-Show," a label they would forget when the pineapple express struck with a vengeance in February. When this "regime change" in the jet stream finally occurred, El Niño's effects in the Pacific Northwest became more favorable. The rest of the winter was warmer and drier than usual, though not to the point of drought. Bulbs flowered early and honeybee populations exploded, bolstering these two important sectors of the region's agricultural economy.

In the Southwest, El Niño's extra moisture, brought there by the altered subtropical jet, had a more benign effect than on the Pacific coast. The additional rainfall was, in fact, welcomed by Arizona after three drought years. In that state and in New Mexico residents were treated to a rare verdancy in the desert as vegetation thrived with the excess rain. Arizona also had economic reasons to embrace the changes wrought by El Niño: The additional rainfall in California was enough to damage and destroy much of that state's multimillion-dollar lettuce crop; Arizona, which boasts the second-highest lettuce crop yield after California, stepped in to meet the shortfall and stepped up lettuce crop production dramatically to meet the growing demand. The additional rainfall in Arizona from El Niño was such that the lettuce crop was not damaged and in many cases benefited, leaving most of Arizona's farmers with a very profitable year.

To the mountainous West, however, an area that

was punished by heavy rains and attendant flooding during the previous "El Niño of the Century" in 1982–83, El Niño 1997–98 engendered a decided dearth of rainfall. In Montana, Wyoming, and Colorado winter precipitation fell off sharply. By February 1998, Montana's snowpack was about 77 percent of normal, prompting Governor Marc Racicot to warn of drought in the spring, when reservoirs depend on the runoff from snowpack melt. Montana's wheat crop was also endangered by El Niño drought, with planters sowing early to take advantage of any moisture they might find during the traditionally wet season and biting their fingernails through an extended dry period that continued into June, damaging much of the crop.

Governor Racicot also expressed fears that the state's parched forests would be increasingly susceptible to fire as spring turned into summer. These fears began to be realized in mid-May, when a number of flare-ups throughout the state signaled a menacingly early start to the forest fire season. Among the first was a blaze that destroyed 220 acres while it raged through highlands some fifty miles north of Missoula. The fire began in a heavily logged section of forest owned by a timber company. Fed by the loose and highly flammable debris and underbrush that is the detritus of industrial logging it gathered strength and soon spread to destroy majestic stands of evergreens in national forest land. It was an ominous har-

binger of a fire season that threatened to equal that of
the terrible years, such as 1988 and 1996, when tens
of thousands of fires burned millions of acres in Montana.

The Midwest

Unseasonably warm temperatures posed less threat in
less heavily forested states such as those in the Midwest and around the Great Lakes. As ABC News reported in February 1998, "In Midwest, El Niño is
Amigo." Temperatures in the fifties had residents of
Minneapolis, Chicago, and Milwaukee pursuing summer recreation such as golfing and tennis in a month
when temperatures are more often in the teens. The
warm weather El Niño brought to the Midwest also
spurred retail activity and saved families and businesses billions of dollars in heating-oil costs (almost
$1\frac{1}{2}$ billion dollars in January alone). This, along with
a diminished likelihood of spring floods because of
scant winter snowfall, comprised the upside of El
Niño, bringing the Midwest its warmest winter in
history.

There was, however, a downside as well. One obvious counterpoint to Midwesterners' enjoyment of
spring and summer recreation in the middle of winter
was a proportionate decline in the fortunes of those
who depend on winter tourism for their livelihoods.
Those involved with cross-country and downhill ski-

ing, snowmobiling, and ice fishing had an economically disastrous season. Farm forecasters also feared the potentially far-reaching effects that could spring from an El Niño–inspired drought in the nation's breadbasket. The 1982–83 and 1987–88 El Niños had a devastating effect on harvests, driving up prices worldwide on grain and other of the region's agricultural exports. The region braced itself for much of the same in 1998, planting crops early as did Montana's wheat farmers. In the end, there was indeed a falloff in production due to reduced rainfall but drought conditions did not take hold to the degree feared.

It is worth noting that El Niño did not suppress winter entirely in the region. We should always bear in mind that even where its influence is strongest, El Niño merely favors certain weather—dry, warm conditions in the Midwest and Great Lakes region—and does not make conditions contrary to those favored by El Niño impossible. Nor does the occurrence of, say, a severe cold snap on Lake Michigan mean that El Niño has lost its power. We look at the larger sampling group of a season's worth of weather to determine how El Niño influences the weather in a given region.

Just such a cold snap did in fact take place in the Midwest in the middle of March 1998. Much of Indiana, Iowa, and Nebraska were subject to record low temperatures and heavy snowfall on the twelfth and thirteenth of the month. Lake Michigan flooded and crushed a seawall in Indiana, destroying dozens of homes and causing millions of dollars of damage. Temperatures of −21°F and −24°F were recorded in Nebraska and Iowa, respectively.

The Southeast

The cold temperatures and heavy precipitation that struck the Midwest in March 1998 were part of a huge storm system that extended up from the South and eventually worked its way into western New York and Pennsylvania. In South Carolina and Georgia, record low temperatures imperiled peach crops at a critical period in their growth. The trees had been coaxed into early bloom by a warm spell and were thus particularly susceptible to the severe cold that took hold in the early part of the month. Particularly hard hit were peach crops in eastern South Carolina, where some growers reported that the cold destroyed up to 90 percent of the premature blossoms. This was alarming news for the nation's peach harvest, given that South Carolina (with an annual harvest worth thirty-five million dollars) lies just behind California in peach production; a large number of unopened buds—less vulnerable to cold—saved the harvest and kept prices stable, however.

All-time lows across the region—28°F in Mobile, Alabama; 47°F at Miami Beach, Florida; 25°F in Montgomery, Alabama; 16°F in Louisville, Kentucky—damaged numerous other fruit crops, as well, including onions and blueberries in Georgia. The large nursery business in these states was also hard hit by the cold. This kind of harsh weather was less of an anomaly in the Southeast than it was in the Midwest during the El Niño winter of 1997–98.

In Georgia, the mid-March cold snap was accompanied by severe flooding and tornadoes. The damage was such that President Clinton declared Georgia a major disaster area on March 11. In March alone, FEMA, the Federal Emergency Management Agency, delivered more than two million dollars of aid to the Georgia victims of El Niño's wrath.

Like California's residents, denizens of the Southeast regarded forecasts of El Niño bringing cold and rain to their region as mostly hype when these conditions had failed to materialize by January 1998. But in the middle of February, at about the same time that the pineapple express began sending punishing storms into the California coast, El Niño struck Dixie with a vengeance. As Tom Matheson, a National Weather Service meteorologist in Wilmington, South Carolina, told the Associated Press, "People were laughing at El Niño before; it's no joke now."

The Carolinas were especially hard hit by mid-February storms. A fishing vessel was lost off Cape Hatteras, killing four; on land, high winds uprooted trees, damaging homes and causing widespread power outages. Wilmington exceeded its record rainfall for February well before the end of the month. Coastal areas such as Myrtle Beach, South Carolina, were flooded to the point that those residents who were able to stay in their homes traveled back and forth from them by canoe or rowboat. In Atlanta, violent hailstorms were to blame for a number of automobile deaths, while high winds claimed at least one life in Florida.

The mid-February storms continued through to the end of the month; the storms that brought flooding in Georgia and record cold throughout the South in mid-March also continued to the end of that month. In Florida, the Suwannee River, which runs down from southern Georgia to eventually drain the Okefenokee swamp, rose to an all-time high before the month was over. River towns throughout the northern half of the state were subjected to a historic torrent of floodwater up to three feet deep that smashed plumbing, fouled electrical lines, and ruined the ground floors of houses.

In Florida's Everglades, Lake Okeechobee rose to a new seasonal high. Flooding throughout this fragile wilderness killed trees and destroyed nesting sites for several species of endangered birds. The whole state was deluged in March with some of the worst flooding occurring in Tampa, where rising waters forced hundreds from their homes while inflicting nearly five million dollars' worth of damage. By month's end, State Agriculture Commissioner Bob Crawford put El Niño's damage to Florida's agriculture at the one-hundred-million-dollar mark. This tally took its place alongside the millions of dollars in lost tourism from a winter in which the Sunshine State had four straight months of record rainfall.

The "Ides of April" proved just as treacherous to the South as had mid-February and mid-March. On April 15 and 16, a line of severe thunderstorms ravaged northern Tennessee and Arkansas as well as southern Illinois. The system, noteworthy for its ferocity even in the 1997–98 El Niño season, brought high winds, hail, torrential downpours, and tornadoes to locales up and down the Ohio and Mississippi River valleys.

In Mississippi County, Arkansas, a tornado killed three and injured twenty while damaging hundreds of homes and downing trees and power lines. A number of tornadoes were also reported in Tennessee. They caused less widespread damage than the one in Arkansas but were nonetheless responsible for two fatalities. In Illinois, the story was much the same, with a rash of twisters reported in several counties. The tornadoes there destroyed a number of homes and left many without power but did not kill anybody.

Just a week before, though, twisters ripping through Alabama killed more than thirty-five people and injured hundreds more in the deadliest bout of tornadoes the state had seen since 1950. Jefferson

County, in the middle of the state, was hardest hit, with more than three hundred homes destroyed and nearly five hundred more damaged.

El Niño and Tornadoes

The United States' deadliest tornado season in years intensified speculation regarding El Niño's role in tornado formation. Scientists have for some time gone back and forth on this issue, some holding that El Niño actually suppresses tornadoes, others claiming the opposite. There does, however, seem to be some consensus in the meteorological community that El Niño brings an earlier tornado season to the United States.

Scientists point to the myriad conditions needed for tornado formation as the reason that it does not make much sense to look at El Niño as the only or primary cause for a specific tornado or series of tornadoes. El Niño does, however, foster a number of conditions that encourage twister formation, thus rendering El Niño, in most scientists' opinions, a secondary or tertiary factor in contributing to the incidence of tornadoes. Certainly El Niño encourages the formation of violent storms; when conditions are optimal, these storms in turn give rise to twisters.

El Niño's shifting of the polar and subpolar jet streams may also have contributed to the high death toll during the 1998 tornado season. Tornado death counts are more or less a matter of chance, but it is worth noting that the change in the jet streams engendered by El Niño causes the primary area of tornado formation to move southward from the Midwest's sparsely populated "tornado alley" to a more populous stretch that cuts across the South's lower tier.

So while most of the tornadoes seen in 1998 can be attributed to El Niño only indirectly—ideal conditions for twister formation were brought about by individual storms that may or may not have happened without El Niño's influence—we may look at the tornadoes that struck central Florida on February 23, 1998, as perhaps the clearest evidence of El Niño's culpability. We tend to think of El Niño as being responsible for these tornadoes because both their timing and placement point to trends encouraged by El Niño. Late February is still well before the tornado season generally begins. And, as we noted in the opening chapter, these particularly intense tornadoes formed right under the new path of a subtropical jet stream that El Niño had both strengthened and steered from its usual course.

El Niño's fingerprints are to be found, therefore, all over the deadliest tornado in a season of deadly tornadoes. These storms, you will recall, were centered around the town of Kissimmee, which lies well to the north of where tornadoes usually strike in Florida. The tornadoes were unusually strong for any part of Florida, bearing winds blowing upward of two hundred miles per hour. The twisters killed forty-two people and injured hundreds more. They destroyed over eight hundred homes and rendered more than seven hundred more uninhabitable. More than three thousand additional residences were damaged at least to some extent. In the course of about an hour in the middle of the night, the tornadoes caused nearly seventy-five million dollars' worth of damage.

The human tragedy was, of course, most poignant. Transcripts of calls to the 911 operator in the Orange County sheriff's office, later published in the *Orlando Sentinel,* graphically illustrate the wholesale devastation and bloody confusion brought by the storms:

Caller: I live at Country Gardens. There's been some kind of accident outside my complex. I hear a lot of crying and carrying on. I don't know what . . .

911: What area of town are you in?

Caller: Winter Garden.

911: OK. We've had a tornado that touched down in there. . . .

Caller: There's a lot of people standing out there, and somebody's screaming and crying.

911: OK. We've got the fire department and sheriff's deputies on the way. . . . Like I said, we had a tornado that touched down in there.

Caller: Oh, my God.

The Northeast

If it can be said that any part of the country got off easily during El Niño, it is the Northeast. Because of the way El Niño shrugs the subpolar jet stream—which usually brings winter storms to the country's northern tier—to the north, meteorologists forecast that the winter would be a mild one in the Northeast, but they did not expect the region to have its warmest winter on record. A particularly warm spell at the end of March brought all-time high temperatures to Washington, D.C.; Wilmington, Delaware; New York City; Philadelphia; and Baltimore. The region was spared billions in heating and highway snow-removal costs, and as in the Midwest, the relatively balmy weather aided the retail economy. Also mirroring the experience of the Midwest was the economic give-and-take between spring- and summer-oriented leisure industries and those aimed at winter activities. With a much greater dependence on winter tourism, though, the Middle Atlantic States and New England lost much more than did the Midwest in a poor season for skiing and other winter sports.

In a winter wherein New York City experienced a historic dearth of snowfall, just about the only rough patch occurred in early January in upstate New York and Maine. We might not blame El Niño for a single bout of extreme weather—particularly as it encourages mild winter weather in the Northeast—except for the fact that, as with February's tornadoes in central Florida, El Niño's fingerprints were all over this case. El Niño makes a strong suspect because irregularities in the jet stream and excess atmospheric moisture—both hallmarks of El Niño—were the key players in this bout of severe weather.

As we saw in chapter 2, the subtropical jet flared northward on January 7, 1998, putting warm, moisture-laden air from the south on a collision course with the much colder subpolar jet that had briefly wandered farther south than is usual in an El Niño year. The collision of warm and cold air and so much moisture was a sure recipe for disaster. The initial result, on January 7, was a deadly ice storm. Once temperatures stabilized, the region was still left with an abundance of moisture that had originated in the Mississippi and Ohio River valleys. Ten days of heavy rain, snow, and flooding followed. If the region was going to have only one major storm system all winter, this was a pretty impressive one to have. In addition to the nine people killed in the ice storm, damage from flooding and ice totaled in the tens of millions of dollars.

The New York ice storm of January 7, 1998, serves to illustrate that even if scientists can paint a general picture of how an El Niño will play out in a given area there is no way they can predict all the individual twists and turns its composite meteorological events will take from one moment to the next. If the

United States had learned from past El Niños to face the 1997–98 episode and its patchwork of effects across the country with an unprecedented degree of readiness, we learned from this most recent El Niño that there is no way to fully guard life and property from a system that is so very massive in scope and so inherently volatile.

6

Ground Zero: Peru and the Pacific

In chapter 2, we saw how El Niño's effects are felt just as acutely in the western Pacific as they are in the east. For every El Niño, though, there is a ground zero: a spot, usually off the South American coast, where the warmest ocean water is concentrated. During the El Niño of 1997–98, ground zero was the Peruvian city of Piura, just over five hundred miles from the capital city of Lima. That most devastating of all El Niños saved some of its very worst for its home turf, hitting Piura like a bull's-eye and radiating destruction up and down the Pan-American Highway, which passes through the town.

Over a span of a few months in 1998, giant convection clouds forming over El Niño's hot waters dumped rainfall measurable in feet onto a region that usually gets mere inches of rain annually. The swollen Piura River washed away the city's largest bridge, sending two buses, a car, and numerous pedestrians into the raging waters below. A search for survivors turned up nothing but scores of dead bodies.

Misery was compounded upon misery as El Niño rains contributed to the crash of a Peruvian air force unit evacuating those left homeless and stranded in the floods. The plane crashed into one of the city's poorest quarters, a jumble of makeshift dwellings already rendered nearly uninhabitable by the flooding. Twenty-eight people were killed.

The same rains that visited an unaccustomed lushness onto the desert surrounding the city have altered the topography closer to shore, as two lagoons spilled over to form a new lake over fifty miles long, which locals have taken to calling La Niña. Such is the force of El Niño and its suffocating grip upon this country; as one frequent traveler on the Pan-American Highway stated with grim directness, "It is no longer Peru since El Niño came."

From Ica in the south, where the flooding of the Ica River left 10 dead and 185,000 homeless, to Trujillo in the north, where an inundated cemetery disinterred 123 coffins and corpses to float down city streets, Peru was battered mercilessly by El Niño 1997–98. Warm ocean waters and the rains they engendered remade the landscape, killed hundreds of people, left hundreds of thousands homeless, and shattered the nation's economy.

The nation that christened El Niño has of course had more than its share of misery from the weather system over the ages. The 1997–98 episode brought back bad memories of the winter of 1982–83, when arid coastal regions received upward of eleven feet of rain. Similarly, the most recent El Niño dumped more than twenty-six times the usual rainfall on the northern town of Tumbes. Residents waded through waters at waist height.

The damage visited upon Peru's stretch of the Pan-American Highway told the story most eloquently. This conduit for the lifeblood of the nation's economy was flooded in over thirty places. Once a source of national pride, it became a gauntlet of water, mud, and truck-sized holes for hundreds of truckers desperate to deliver their rotting wares and for thousands of miserable refugees of El Niño's fury. Throughout the country, over sixty bridges were washed away by floods, almost six hundred miles of highway destroyed, and close to four thousand miles of road were badly damaged.

In Lima, Peru's capital, the storms foreshadowed the political turmoil that El Niño would also bring. In the city's outskirts, the working-class community of Campoy was flooded by the Apurimac River, which had been dry for years. Torrential rains not only restored the flow of water to the dry river bed, they quickly caused it to exceed its old banks.

Elsewhere in the sprawling town, the Huaycolor River flooded its banks as well, sending three feet of water washing through city streets. Only a heroic sandbagging effort prevented the floods from reaching historic Acho Plaza. Not spared, however, were hundreds of shacks that some of Lima's poorer residents called home. Many of Lima's oldest buildings also fell prey to the rains over time, their adobe foundations crumbling. Chan Chan, the world's largest adobe city, covered its buildings in plastic to prevent them from becoming just so much mud.

Campoy and other stricken communities in the capital became the focal point for a concerted relief effort. President Fujimori, who visited the areas hardest hit and offered what comfort he could, wished also to send the message that Peru could take care of itself.

It was a message intended to buttress Fujimori's claim that the cost of getting aid to devastated areas of the country would not pose a challenge to the national budget. The President's political opponents, however, hotly contested his damage estimate of 800 million dollars. They supplied the vastly larger sum of 1.8 billion dollars as more realistic and accused Fujimori of playing politics with the country's well-being. The opposition branded the well-publicized relief efforts as paltry and demanded more be done—

to clothe and feed the hundreds of thousands of homeless; to shore up sodden building foundations, river banks, and levees; to dig out towns and neighborhoods buried under flowing mud; and, in a huge challenge to Peru's health care community, to forestall the kind of cholera and malaria epidemics that had followed El Niño's flooding in the past. Overflowing sewage systems and stagnant water provide the perfect breeding grounds for deadly bacteria and disease-carrying mosquitoes. During El Niño in 1991, some 3,000 people died out of more than 200,000 who fell ill with cholera.

For Fujimori's government, there was more at issue than relief efforts and the money allocated in the budget to pay for them. The 1997–98 El Niño struck at a particularly cruel time for a nation that had just begun to make substantial economic headway after decades of great poverty. Fujimori's government had, since taking office, encouraged a great deal of foreign investment in Peru that, combined with a degree of good fortune, had seen the Peruvian economy grow an impressive 7.6 percent in 1997. The advent of El Niño spelled the end of that prosperous period as growth dipped to a torpid 2 percent in 1998.

The wholesale destruction of the nation's highway system was of course a huge blow. Food and other perishables rotted or were simply washed away by floods. Producers, processors, markets, consumers all suffered from this great waste of resources. President

Fujimori, in an attempt to mitigate the loss, ordered navy vessels to ship fruits and vegetables bound from the northern port of Paiti to the capital city.

The retail economy began to stagger as early as the Peruvian winter of 1997 (Peru, being in the Southern Hemisphere, experiences winter while we have summer, and vice versa), when unusually high temperatures left winter clothes virtually untouched on store shelves and in great open air bazaars such as Lima's Malvinas market. One merchant there told *USA Today* of El Niño's effect on the textile trade with a succinctness that belied her desperation: "Winter never came. Sales are down 80 percent. I'm going broke."

It should come as no surprise by now that El Niño's warm waters once again exacted a huge toll on Peru's anchovy fisheries. Those fish that survived the reduced upwelling of nutrients from below migrated north to more favorable waters. In Chimbote, the heart of Peru's fishing industry, catches fell from a daily total of twenty-five million tons to barely five million tons a day. With the passage of a moratorium on fishing in January 1998, anchovy processing, like the sales of the clothes merchant above, dropped by almost 80 percent.

Fish weren't the only marine life endangered by El Niño. Just offshore of Lima, the one-two punch of battering storms and the depletion of the fish upon which they fed had, by February 1998, led to 50 percent losses in sea lion colonies. Efforts to rescue stranded newborn sea lions met with mixed success; by the end of March, less than 20 percent of the original population remained alive.

The Blast Radius: South America Reels

Peru, at ground zero, is not the only nation in South and Central America that El Niño hits hard. The 1997–98 El Niño had, in the straightforward words of Robert Gay, director of Latin American research at the Banker's Trust investment bank, an "economic impact on South America [that was] negative, and in some parts it [was] disastrous, especially [in] the Andean countries."

The Andes mountains continue south from Peru into Chile. Chile, a thin strip of a nation, only two hundred miles across at its widest, follows the long mountain chain that forms its eastern boundary down to South America's southern tip. Chile, then, is the southernmost nation in the Western Hemisphere to feel El Niño's effects. It is also a country that feels these effects so directly and reliably that it is considered, along with Peru, an ideal subject for El Niño case studies.

A recent study by three scientists at the Center for Ocean-Atmospheric Prediction Studies (COAPS) at Florida State University showed that, in El Niño years, precipitation in northern and central Chile in-

creases by an average of about 20 percent. The 1997–
98 El Niño exceeded that average in most areas and
the result was, as in Peru, a disaster for the economy
and for life and limb.

The heaviest economic blow came from a collapse
of Chilean fisheries similar to what had happened in
Peru. As for danger to people, the heavy rains
brought not only deadly floods but an unusually
abundant bloom of bamboo, which led in turn to an
explosion of the rat population. Incidence of the
deadly Hantavirus, a disease spread through rodent
feces, increased dramatically.

The small coastal nation of Ecuador lies less than
one hundred miles to the north of Piura, El Niño's
ground zero. Accordingly, it is more directly affected
by El Niño than many parts of Peru. Floods and mud
slides killed 161 people and left 20,000 homeless in
1997–98; by the time the 1997–98 El Niño had run
its course, flooding had caused well over two billion
dollars' damage to the nation's roads, bridges, and
rail lines. In mid-March, persistent rain triggered a
landslide that fractured Ecuador's largest oil pipeline.
The resulting explosion and fire near the northern
port of Esmereldas killed seventeen people and left
seventy-four more badly burned. The incident was
also an ecological disaster, as roughly eight thousand
barrels of crude oil surged from the broken pipeline
into a nearby river. Ecuador's oil-dependent economy
also suffered when the blaze interrupted the flow of

oil from the Lake Agra oil field in the country's interior.

The agricultural sector of the Ecuadorian economy also suffered greatly during the 1997–98 El Niño, with some 300,000 acres destroyed by rains that also prevented farmers from planting an additional half million acres. The nation's banana plantations, producers of Ecuador's most important agricultural export, were decimated by flooding. By the end of the rainiest period in March almost 40,000 acres of banana plantation lay under stagnant, muddy water. Twelve percent of the crop was destroyed.

El Niño's calamities, combined with a reduced worldwide price for crude oil, dealt crippling blows to the Ecuadorian economy, prompting President Fabian Alarcon to enact in mid-March a variety of emergency measures designed to keep it from collapsing altogether. Included in the package was a significant tax hike to help pay for repairs to the country's infrastructure.

Human suffering was also great. In Milagro, peasants fashioned makeshift huts along the main road. These refugees of El Niño were seeking the only shelter and high ground they could find, either afraid or unable to return to their small farms until the rains again let up. There was a sense of abandonment among those left bereft by flooding, especially as diseases such as dengue, malaria, and cholera began to crop up in epidemic proportions in roadside camps such as these. As one peasant complained to the Associated Press in March 1998, "No one has brought us anything—not a drop of milk or piece of bread—for two weeks. It's clear we don't matter to them." As she said this, her bare feet, caked in mud and infected with fungus growing rampant in the incessant moisture, seemed to confirm her suspicions.

Over the Andes: Brazil and the Interior

El Niño's storms do not only affect those nations along South America's west coast. In the South American interior, Brazil also falls prey to El Niño's anomalous weather conditions as high-altitude winds intensified by the phenomenon bring coastal moisture over the Andes. Because of Brazil's great size, however, El Niño's manifestations in that country take different forms according to region.

In Brazil's southern region, rainfall is typically far above normal in an El Niño year. Such was the forecast of Brazil's civil defense bureau for the areas surrounding São Paulo, Mato Grosso do Sul, and the whole of the country's south for the period of March through July 1998. And rainfall far above normal was precisely what Brazil got for that period.

The heavy rains began to fall, however, in October 1997. By late in the month, severe flooding had left some twenty thousand people homeless. Hardest hit was the community of Itaqui in the state of Rio

Grande do Sul, where the Uruguay River had flooded almost 10 feet (3 meters) over its banks. Damage to homes and farms was widespread throughout southern Brazil, with states of emergency declared in nearly one hundred of the region's counties. By January 1998 the months of flooding had led to a mosquito-spread dengue epidemic. Incidence of the disease was seven times that of the previous year. Acres of the nation's key sugar and tobacco crops lay under water. When the traditional rainy season arrived in March, southern Brazil's sodden misery only deepened.

In the country's north, however, a very different picture generally unfolds during El Niño. Like Mexico and parts of Central America, El Niño often brings drought to northern Brazil. Once again, the 1997–98 El Niño brought the expected dose of disaster, and then some. The drought that stifled the rainy season in 1998 was the worst in twenty-five years. Of more lasting concern than the serious crop failure the drought caused was the role the drought played in accelerating fires that tore through untouched sections of the Amazon rain forest. Some 10 percent of the two-million-square-mile rain forest was destroyed by these fires, according to most estimates.

The drought brought by El Niño 1997–98 also fed forest fires in Colombia, one of Brazil's neighbors to the north. Its effect on this nation's agriculture was devastating as well, causing a nearly 10 percent drop in farm production and hitting Colombia's vital coffee crop particularly hard. The drought did not only cause these predictable calamities along South America's northern ridge, however. The minute nation of Guyana had its economy scuttled when streams used to traffic gold mined deep in the jungle dried up. Production nearly ground to a halt, down by nearly 40 percent during El Niño. In Venezuela a similar decrease in river flow forced hydroelectric plants to resort to the unusual step of power rationing.

Farther North: A Zone of Drought

Looking north, El Niño's warm waters did some very direct harm to vital marine life off Panama's Pacific coast. Sea-surface temperatures in the region were, by spring 1998, nearly 2 degrees Celsius higher than is the norm. This excess warmth bleached coral in reefs that are home to thousands of species of fish, crustaceans, and mollusks. The coral in this area does best when temperatures are at 29 degrees Celsius or below; with temperatures climbing over 31 degrees and remaining there for months, it is estimated that up to 90 percent of the coral suffered substantial damage, some of which may be permanent. Luckily, though, the bleaching off Panama was less intense than it was during the 1982–83 El Niño.

In southern North America, similar conditions prevailed. The 1997–98 El Niño encouraged the formation of a massive high-pressure system over central Mexico. The dry, cool temperatures that resulted proved deadly to many and sent shock waves through a nation already on shaky economic footing.

In December 1998 record-setting cold and snowfall began to take hold in Mexico, when temperatures in Chihuahua dropped to −11 degrees Fahrenheit, killing twenty. Meanwhile, in Guadalajara, sixteen inches of snow fell, which was not only the most in more than one hundred years, but the first snowfall there since 1881, a year that saw unprecedented cold worldwide.

An unusually harsh winter continued to punish a nation unaccustomed to nature's fury coming in such a chilly form. In early February, snow fell in ten Mexican states while high winds ripped apart homes, killing three. By June, however, drought conditions engendered by the high-pressure system were creating a different sort of problem: fires that raged out of control through south-central Mexico's tropical rain forests.

The fires sent thick clouds of smoke and haze over the border to the United States, fouling air as far north as Wisconsin and as far east as Georgia. This drop in air quality, however, was but the most visible aspect for the United States of what scientists and developmental specialists throughout the world were terming a major environmental disaster. Brian Atwood, head of the Agency for International Development, called the situation in Mexico "the most serious of its kind we have seen anywhere in the world, including the fires in Indonesia."

After touring the Chimalapas rain forest, the hardest hit area, with the United States Agriculture Secretary Dan Glickman, Atwood expressed great concern for the loss of biodiversity the fires could cause. With at least 1,500 of the world's most endangered species of plant life growing in the Chimalapas and 130 of the 150 most-used pharmaceuticals in the United States dependent on ingredients gathered from the forest, the fires represented not only a grave threat to the world's environment but to human health as well. When one factors in the amazing statistic that up to 90 percent of the birds that migrate to the United States use the Chimalapas as an important stop on their migratory route, one begins to appreciate that the fires were another adverse effect of El Niño for the United States, as well as a catastrophe for Mexico.

Fighting the fires was made extremely difficult because of their tendency to spread along forest underbrush while leaving tree canopies intact. This made the fires very difficult to spot and fight from the air, a method generally crucial to combating large-scale forest fires. The extremely remote location of the fires also made fighting them on land a very difficult proposition. And with drought conditions persisting throughout the summer of 1998, little help was available in the form of rain from above.

By midsummer 1998 well over a hundred fires continued to burn, some of the almost 15,000 total seen in the Mexican rain forests during that year. In the end, nearly one million acres of rain forest were lost in Mexico. Gone up in smoke were irreplaceable resources in one of the planet's great treasure houses of environmental diversity on land. The scope of the disaster reaches even further, however, when we consider that the rain forests act essentially as the planet's lungs, converting huge volumes of carbon dioxide into the oxygen vital for all life on earth. Not only were a major portion of these "lungs" eaten away by fires in Mexico, Brazil, Honduras, Nicaragua, Guatemala, El Salvador, and Costa Rica—all within El Niño's drought zone—but the fires themselves greatly raised the levels of so-called greenhouse gases in the atmosphere, challenging the portion of the earth's lungs that remained.

In March 1998, in what can only be regarded by man as a huge cautionary flag laid down by Mother Nature, migratory monarch butterflies, felled by the forest fires and record cold, lay on the forest floor, a carpet of dead beauty more than a foot deep.

7

The Other Side of the Coin: Drought Down Under and in Asia

Meanwhile, on the other side of the Pacific, El Niño's effects are similar to those in Mexico, Central America, and northern South America but dramatically different from those at the ground zero region of Peru, Ecuador, and Chile. The eastward migration of storm-cloud concentration and the interruption of the Walker Circulation by El Niño can leave Australia, Southeast Asia, India, large stretches of China, and the many island groups of the western and South Pacific high and dry. In the El Niño of 1997–98, this is exactly what happened, with devastating consequences that mirrored those across the Pacific: loss of life, economic catastrophe, and dire, possibly far-reaching, environmental damage.

If Piura, Peru, could be thought of as ground zero for El Niño 1997–98 because it abutted the warmest ocean waters, Australia must be regarded as the central point of impact for the high-pressure system that sits over the western Pacific in the El Niño phase of the Southern Oscillation. Australia and the islands of the western Pacific are those most consistently stricken by earth-cracking drought when El Niño holds sway. This effect was certainly evident during the El Niño of 1982–83, as we saw in chapter 3. It was also painfully manifest during the 1997–98 episode.

Australia: Dry Earth, Fire, and Hot Water

As in the 1982–83 El Niño, brushfires were again a major threat to Australia's population and wildlife in the 1997–98 El Niño. In the fall of 1997, they raged through a number of regions, encouraged by drought, heat, and high winds. These fires broke out on a vast scale in mid-October, burning an area the size of England in western Australia's far outback. By November 26 lightning had touched off a rash of similar fires in the country's south. Sixty-mile-per-hour winds swept the fires through parched brush and forest, causing widespread devastation. No relief came from skies where the only clouds were those of smoke from the fires below. Temperatures hit 115 degrees Fahrenheit and did not fall below 104 degrees for several days. By Christmas, rampant brushfires and the fear of additional conflagrations scuttled traditional barbecue plans across the country. By December it also became clear that drought had taken a toll on the nation's wheat harvest.

The 1997–98 El Niño was accompanied by significant warming of Australia's and New Zealand's coastal waters. The degree to which El Niño caused or exacerbated these conditions remains a matter of scientific debate but there seems to be some consensus that El Niño played at least a part. Whatever the degree of El Niño's role in these warm waters, a wide spectrum of marine life suffered from the change. In November 1997 two different species of seals washed ashore in New Zealand in disturbing numbers. Most of them, already near death from starvation and disease, were put to sleep. Aquatic birds such as the brown noddie were also affected adversely by the way the high ocean temperatures disrupted the area's food chain.

It was in February 1998, however, that the region's marine life took its biggest hits. Early in the month, starvation and an unidentified disease killed 53 percent of New Zealand's sea lion pups and 20 percent of adult sea lions, with the greatest losses in the ecologically rich Auckland Islands. Next came a deadly algal bloom off of New Zealand's east coast. Earlier in the year there had been fears in Australia that a similar bloom would adversely affect the continent-nation's supply of drinking water by taking hold in reservoirs and lakes. The bloom in New Zealand, being in the ocean rather than inland, inflicted further losses on the region's population of marine mammals by killing a large number of seals. Crustaceans and mollusks such as rock lobster, crayfish, and octopus were also victims of the bloom. New Zealand's Great Barrier Island was closed to shellfishing.

Of potentially greater long-term concern, however, is what happened to Australia's Great Barrier Reef during that same month. This coral reef has been described as the ocean's rain forest. It is comprised of a great mass of skeletal and living coral that provide both shelter and oxygen to an amazingly large and diverse population of marine life. Though the largest reef of its kind, it is, like the imperiled coral off the Panamanian coast we encountered in chapter 6, a large but fragile ecosystem, extremely sensitive to fluctuations in temperature. The coral in the Great Barrier Reef does best in ocean waters no hotter than 28 degrees Celsius (82 degrees Fahrenheit); higher temperatures can cause bleaching that is potentially fatal to the coral.

With ocean temperatures hitting 86 degrees in February and remaining there for an extended period, a great deal of bleaching occurred. The sea-surface temperatures of Australia's coastal waters climbed significantly higher during the 1997–98 El Niño

than they did during even the colossal 1982–83 episode; only time will tell if this oddity caused irrepara-
ble damage to the Great Barrier Reef and, by
extension, the planet.

Oceania's Islands: Water, Water Everywhere . . .

The islands of the western Pacific, a part of the world
known to geographers as Oceania, are as directly influenced by El Niño as is Australia. These many, tiny
isles often lack the sort of sophisticated infrastructure
that allows many countries to cope, however imper-
fectly, with interruptions in supplies of food and water. Frequently isolated by miles of ocean, life hangs
in a precarious balance easily upset by the whims of
nature.

One island chain that is well equipped to deal with
extreme drought is that which comprises our fiftieth
state, the Hawaiian Islands. Hawaii nonetheless suffered through the 1997–98 El Niño, its worst ever.
From January 1998 to well into June, Hawaii lived
under a constant state of drought-induced emergency.
Hardest hit was the island of Hawaii itself, known to
locals as the Big Island. Its parched vegetation flared
up in a rash of over one hundred wildfires beginning
in March. Neighboring islands Maui and Oahu were
similarly afflicted.

The islands' agriculture was predictably hard hit,
with farmers experiencing losses of 20 to 100 per-

cent, depending on their crop. Hawaii was once again the island where the effect was the worst. It also had to deal with a shortage of drinking water used by many rural families while playing host to the largest volume of tourists.

Less well equipped to deal with crushing drought was the tiny Federated States of Micronesia, a loose geographical cluster of more than a thousand islands some eight hundred miles northwest of Papua New Guinea. Micronesia's harrowing experience during the 1997–98 El Niño is perhaps a more typical one among Pacific islands than that of Hawaii's. As such it merits a closer look here.

Kent M. Ainslie, a Peace Corps medical officer in the Micronesian state of Pohnpei, remembers when he first noticed El Niño taking hold. One day in December, he saw that several of the small stands of tapioca plants near his office had lost some of their lower leaves. The ground was dry and there hadn't been a good rain in quite some time.

This was unusual indeed for the 130-square-mile island of Pohnpei, which generally has the type of weather meteorologists term "maritime tropical." The people who live there, however, might simply call it, as Dr. Ainslie puts it, "hot, humid, and wet, very wet!" Rain falls on the island some three hundred days in an average year. December's rainfall, however, totaled a mere eight inches, only half the norm.

By January, drought conditions had reached a point where the local government declared a state of emergency and convened an El Niño task force to cope with the problem. It was around this time that the other Micronesian states assembled similar task forces of their own. Normal January precipitation levels are about eleven inches; in January 1998 a scant two inches fell from the sky. Signs urging water preservation (even, in a bow to local priorities, one that asked residents to "wash pigs and cars less frequently or not at all") gave way to outright water rationing: one could use water only between the hours of six and nine in the morning and evening.

In the town of Kolonia, five of the six wells the residents depended upon for water dried out, and the closest river, another important water source, got so low that only a quarter of the usual volume of water could be pumped from it each hour. Outside his office, Dr. Ainslie noted with sadness, the tapiocas had now lost half of their leaves. The groundwater source that fed his home had not dried out since the El Niño of 1982–83. It was now reduced to a trickle.

With February's arrival and passage, drought conditions continued in Pohnpei; less than two inches of rain fell against, again, an eleven-inch norm, and residents did what they could to save and obtain water. Those buildings that could tapped into the municipal water supply, creating a booming market for plastic piping. The state El Niño task force organized deliveries of water to remote villages, carried in thousand-gallon tanks on flatbed trucks. By month's end, there were a number of bare stalks among those in Dr. Ainslie's tapioca patch.

In the Micronesian state of Chuuk, El Niño hit even harder. Chuuk was, in fact, the state most affected by drought; on February 5, 1998, the governor declared a state of emergency, which also provided for the creation of a fifteen-person El Niño task force. The task force was similar to that created in Pohnpei and in other states throughout the Federated States of Micronesia. The efforts of these state task forces were coordinated through a national task force. In a country made up of over a thousand islands, logistics could quickly become complicated.

The state of Chuuk alone is comprised of forty inhabited islands, all of which were visited during the 1998 drought by El Niño field teams. Field teams were comprised of people from the Departments of Agriculture and Health, the government's Disaster Central Office, members of the task force, and U.S. Peace Corps volunteers. Over the course of the crisis, field teams made about fifteen trips to the state's various island clusters, each trip involving stops at several islands and lasting about twenty days. By El Niño's end, these relief teams had delivered nearly one million gallons of water by boat to the state's various island groups. With each relief trip costing roughly twelve to sixteen thousand dollars when one factors in the costs of fuel, water, provisions, and labor, the relief effort in Chuuk alone required budgetary allotments of about two million dollars.

Veronica de Aboitiz, a Peace Corps volunteer who was a field team member on a number of these trips, remembered the experience: "It was terrible. No one was dying but it was clear that, without the water we were bringing, it wouldn't have been long before things got really desperate for the people on these islands. There was a simple, dire need for water. The wells that these people used for water were almost uniformly dry by January. In fact, the situation worsened because, as the wells were emptied of fresh water, seawater seeped in with the tides, contaminating the wells. Everywhere we went, the old men of the town would want to sit down and talk to us, see if we had any idea when the rains might come again."

Despite the successful implementation of this well-planned relief effort, the drought dragged and even worsened to the point where, by the end of March, the task force was looking to its mitigation plan: water delivery would continue to those islands where it was most needed while stocks of water would be replenished with the aid of four desalinization plants. The rains finally began to come in late April and early May, however, just as the mitigation plan was nearing implementation. Chuuk was spared having to turn to its last resort.

The involvement of relief groups such as the Peace Corps—in Micronesia's case—underscores the difficulty in delivering relief to nations comprised of islands well removed from one another. The island groups of the relatively poor nation of Papua New Guinea, for instance, required food donations from Australia and New Zealand to prevent famine from accompanying severe drought there.

Asia's Sword of Damocles: El Niño's Threat to the Monsoon

Understanding the dynamic of the Asian monsoon is key to appreciating how El Niño's effects reach far past Australia and the western Pacific to the Indian subcontinent and even to southern Africa. As we saw in chapter 3, the way that El Niño interferes with the arrival of the monsoon throughout the western Pacific and on to India has been a source of concern and impetus for research on the El Niño Southern Oscillation for over a hundred years now.

In a normal year Asia's summer monsoon brings the countries in its path most of their annual rainfall. Beginning roughly in April in China, this seasonal reversal of winds, though known by different names in the nations it touches—in China, it is "Mei-yu"; in Japan, "Baiu"; progressing northward, Koreans know it as "Chang Mau"—is nonetheless universally vital to their economies and health. It brings India, which it typically reaches by late August, some 80 percent of its annual rainfall.

The summer monsoon is not the only one vital to precipitation in Asia, however. The Philippines and Indonesia, as well as parts of Southeast Asia, receive the bulk of their annual rainfall from the northeast monsoon. This monsoon prevails from November through March.

In chapter 2 we saw how the El Niño phase of the Southern Oscillation shifts the rain-producing low-pressure system that the Walker Circulation usually generates over the western Pacific to the east. This low-pressure system also generates the moisture carried across Asia by the monsoons. When it shifts to the east during an El Niño, Australia and the western Pacific are not necessarily the only regions robbed of conditions necessary for rainfall; the areas dependent on monsoonal rains may also be left thirsty.

Indonesia's Toll: Thousands of Acres and One Government

Indonesia, like its neighbor the Philippines, is a frequent victim of drought in El Niño years. Drought has visited its share of misery upon the nation throughout its history. Those living on the islands of Central Java, for instance, still remember the great drought of 1962, when the only food was boiled bark and rats. The 1997–98 El Niño, however, brought this nation of thousands of islands even more than grim drought. The "El Niño of the Century" left the Indonesian economy in tatters and its government teetering on the brink of full-scale revolution.

El Niño 1997–98 did, to be sure, cause drought in Indonesia: crop failure and a dwindling supply of fresh water killed hundreds through famine or out-breaks of diseases such as cholera. Most significantly, however, the extremely dry conditions that prevailed in the area, exacerbated by the failure of the northeast monsoon in November, dried Indonesia's forests and ground vegetation to the point where it was little more than tinder waiting to be set ablaze. Which is exactly what began to happen in September 1997 as vast swaths of forest acreage went up in flames throughout Indonesia. By late in the month, smoke from the fires was so thick as to cause the crash of a Garuda Airlines A-300 Airbus near Sumatra, killing more than 230 people.

By November, smoke from the still-raging fires had found its way to their symbolic point of origin: Darwin, Australia. An 870-mile-long plume of thick smoke reduced visibility in ENSO's western pole to less than one mile at midmonth. The fires burned on into 1998, joining blazes in Malaysia, Singapore, and Thailand in racking up billions of dollars in damage. Decreased visibility off the Malaysian coast brought its own version of the Airbus crash: a cargo ship ran aground, killing twenty-nine.

In addition to the obvious cost of fighting the fires, the soot and particulate they threw into the atmosphere had an adverse effect on tourism, air travel, fishing, and many sectors of Indonesian industry. The hazy air was also a public health nightmare, with incidence of pulmonary disease increasing dramatically after the advent of the fires, and with long-term effects yet to be reckoned.

We should not forget that the severe drought that encouraged and propagated these fires was still very much in effect while they burned their way across Indonesia. Crop failure joined severe drinking-water shortages to compound the country's misery. The vicious circle was joined when the drought-encouraged fires began to exacerbate the drought's effects; in February 1998 ash falling to earth from the fires caused the pH of the water in the Barito River to drop to an acidic 2.5, rendering it unsafe to drink. In the east Kalimantan province, meanwhile, the drought was playing cruel tricks of its own. With river levels at or near all-time lows, seawater crept upriver with the tides, causing saltwater intrusion nearly forty miles upriver in some places, thus making the small amount of water left undrinkable.

It was the fires, however, that had the greatest effect on Indonesia. By March the burning forests had released as much carbon dioxide into the atmosphere as all of Europe generally does in a year. When scientists factored in the secondary and potential long-range effects of the fires, they saw that they had a real environmental catastrophe on their hands. When by April almost half a million acres had been destroyed in the East Kalimantan province and the fires showed no signs of abating, environmental ministers from the nine-nation Association of South East Asian Nations (ASEAN) met to coordinate disaster mitigation efforts.

The ministers realized that immediate action had to be taken because, though El Niño was forecast to end in May, there was still no guarantee of rain in the foreseeable future. As a representative from the Indonesian Environmental Ministry said in an interview with Reuters at the time, "The end of the El Niño phenomenon is not likely to be directly followed by a decrease in the forest fires because we don't know when the rainy season will come." The next monsoon rains would not arrive until about October. To avert disaster from the smoke, haze, and smog that had settled over the region, they devised a plan to concentrate efforts on the worst areas.

The special fire-fighting units dispatched to Kalimantan and Sumatra met with some success in fighting the fires but they had already delivered a crushing blow to the already fragile Indonesian economy, as well as other economies in the region. Indonesia, as a precondition for a large International Monetary Fund loan, took the economically painful step of devaluing its currency in April 1998. The move, when piled on the economic woe that El Niño and the fires had already brought, proved to be the straw that broke the camel's back for the people of Indonesia. In mid-May, demonstrators massed in the capital city of Jakarta succeeded in forcing President Suharto to step down. Suharto was able to name his own successor, however. With the jury still out as to whether the new government represents a real change, it remains to be seen to what degree El Niño has rewritten Indonesia's history.

Asia: Spared the Worst

Across the Asian mainland, a decidedly more mixed picture emerged during the 1997–98 El Niño. China experienced its worst heat wave this century, in which fifty people died in July 1997; in December of that year, the winter monsoon failed, bringing northern China its most severe drought in decades. The winter monsoon is somewhat less vital to the regions to which it brings rains than is the summer monsoon but its failure here nonetheless damaged well over six million acres of winter wheat and exacted even heavier losses on the fall wheat crop. Bangladesh, meanwhile, suffered its most severe cold snap in years in January 1998, while nearby India dodged a bullet when the summer monsoon did not fail in either 1997 or 1998.

Onward to Africa: A Trail of Misery
Ends in Disease

Sir Gilbert Walker, who, as we saw in chapter 3, first
established the Southern Oscillation, observed that,
in addition to the Darwin, Australia–Tahiti pressure
seesaw in ENSO, "there is a tendency of pressure at
stations in the Pacific to increase while pressure in
the region of the Indian Ocean decreases." And, as we
learned in chapter 2, systems of low pressure encourage the creation of rain clouds. For the northeast-
ern African nations of Kenya, Somalia, Ethiopia,
Uganda, and Tanzania, then, El Niño can mean flooding of the sort we saw in South America in the last
chapter. So just as we ended that chapter on the primarily wet conditions in the east with the drought
that prevails in Mexico, we bring this chapter on the
primarily dry conditions on the western side of the
Pacific to a close with African flooding.

Northeast Africa's drenching was made worse in El
Niño 1997–98 by the fact that it was preceded by
drought conditions. This drought, probably also related to El Niño, damaged the coffee crops in Kenya,
Uganda, and Tanzania and the wheat crop in Ethiopia. Kenya's crop of maize, its primary staple, was
pummeled by a one-two of drought while it was
growing and torrential rains at harvest time. Kenya's
sugar, rice, and wheat crops met a similar fate, suffering up to 50 percent shortfalls in yield. Drought not
only dried out crops but the earth as well, leaving it

loose and unable to absorb the sudden quantities of moisture it received once the rains began.

The flooding started in Somalia in November 1997. Three weeks of rain merged the paths of two rivers there, creating an inland ocean and drowning thousands of head of cattle. The flooding also killed a number of people and left five hundred homeless. At the end of the month, additional flooding in Kenya led to an outbreak of diarrhea that claimed twelve lives. It was to prove a grim harbinger of things to come.

In December 1997 and January 1998 all hell broke loose. The flooding in the region had led to the creation of what the World Health Organization would later call a "viral soup"—wet, hot conditions that proved an excellent breeding ground for tropical disease. In the largest-ever outbreak of its kind, 89,000 people in Somalia and Kenya fell ill with Rift Valley fever; some 250 died from the disease. The same number of people also died from a horrific outbreak of hemorrhagic fever in these two countries.

Kenya and Somalia were not the only northeast African countries stricken by epidemics during the floods. In February 1998 a malaria outbreak in Uganda proved so severe as to cause a serious blood shortage. Nor were humans the only victims. In Kenya, up to 30 percent of sheep herds were lost to a blue tongue outbreak, a disease not seen in the region since 1905. Even vultures and hyenas left animal carcasses to rot untouched during this period.

Amid oddities such as an explosion of orange-and-black beetles in Kenya and the flocking of a million and a half flamingos to rain-freshened Lake Nakaru in the Rift Valley, Africa seized for itself the unhappy distinction of being the continent hardest hit by disease during the 1997–98 El Niño. It seemed a cruel fate for Africa; though South Africa was spared the agony of El Niño–inspired drought and famine, the poorest continent was still doled more than its share of suffering.

8

But Wait, There's More: Plagues of Biblical Proportions

El Niño's immediate effects, as we have seen, can be quite dramatic. And when a relentless series of storms so saturates the ground that a mud slide results, or when a full rainy season goes by with scant precipitation for withered crops, it's fairly easy to view El Niño as the culprit. As scientists have become more sophisticated in their understanding of El Niño's far-flung meteorological interactions, however, we as a society have also become increasingly aware of El Niño's less immediate effects.

Among the more pernicious of El Niño's secondary effects are the breeding conditions for disease and all manner of creeping, crawling pests fostered by El Niño's seasons of extreme weather. We have already encountered El Niño's secondary effects in the form of the cholera outbreaks suffered in Peru during the 1991 El Niño (see chapter 6) and the "viral soup" brewed up in Kenya after the 1997–98 El Niño's ceaseless rains (see chapter 7). We have also seen such strange secondary effects as mass hatchings of orange-and-black beetles—again in Africa—and the sobering specter of a Mexican forest floor littered with dead monarch butterflies.

Because the types of organisms that thrive in severe conditions are often those that present the greatest threat to humans—vermin and disease—El Niño's secondary effects are often dangerous and even deadly. They are also fascinating: Barren deserts blooming (to note one of the more benign secondary effects) and city streets aswarm with grasshoppers seem somehow miraculous. Seemingly ceaseless rain and drought followed by such evidence of nature gone awry as presented by these examples combine to form a picture of a force of nearly biblical proportions. Here is a force, these swarms of critters seem to say, that can wreak all sorts of havoc even after it is gone. There is, in fact, some speculation that the drought suffered by Egypt, and described in Exodus, may have been the result of El Niño. Likewise, some wonder if the plague of locusts visited upon the Egyptians may also have been a secondary effect of El Niño.

More than an Annoyance: Swarms of Mosquitoes

The mosquito has been a pest to humankind since time immemorial. And the ability of various mosquito species to spread malaria and other potentially deadly diseases has made this parasite more than a middle-of-the-night annoyance in many parts of the world. Malaria epidemics are a constant health threat in the globe's tropical regions, notably equatorial Africa and the Americas, killing millions every year. The standing water that El Niño rains can leave in these regions provides ideal breeding grounds for malaria-spreading mosquitoes. One of the better known malarial epidemics associated with El Niño occurred during the construction of the Panama Canal in the winter of 1905–06, when scores of those digging the giant trench were killed by the disease.

During the 1997–98 El Niño, the incessant rains that fell on Peru from the first of January began to result in huge increases in the insect population by the beginning of February. The effects of the 1997–98 El Niño were felt earlier in this part of the world than in any other due to the early start the phenomenon got on its home turf. The water under which most of South America found itself, combined with record-breaking heat throughout the region provided mosquitoes, in particular, with perfect breeding conditions. A lack of education in basic health practices and in how to prevent mosquitoes from breeding also made much of Peru's peasantry especially susceptible to the outbreaks of infectious disease borne by the mosquitoes. The conditions were ripe, in other words, for epidemics.

Despite emergency preventive measures ordered by President Fujimori, in those population centers hardest hit by El Niño, such as the ground zero city of Piura, massive hatchings of mosquitoes in the late winter and early spring created a public health crisis that worsened as the spring progressed. The concentration of the disease in certain areas of Peru was brought home chillingly by the words of Rosa Chero, a resident of northern Peru who was interviewed by the BBC: "It started with my youngest baby and then the other two children. Now they are all sick. It could be me next."

The burgeoning mosquito population was also suspected as being responsible for the outbreak of a mysterious fever that killed nearly twenty people in the northern Peruvian cities of Talara, Trujillo, and Chimbote. The disease produced agonizing symptoms of fever, coughing, and diarrhea that could last up to three weeks before victims died.

Meanwhile, in Brazil and Argentina, mass hatchings of a different species of mosquito posed another deadly risk. Again, a combination of El Niño's heavy rains and high temperatures, and the local neglect of key hygienic practices set the stage for an epidemic, this time of dengue fever, a disease with a significantly higher fatality rate than that of malaria. The looming crisis posed by the mosquito swarms reawakened national memories of epidemics that killed thousands in these countries during the early years of the twentieth century.

In Buenos Aires, the Argentine capital, the government undertook a large-scale effort to fumigate public and private buildings. Insecticide was also directed at likely breeding grounds in the Argentinian countryside. The strategy worked to some extent, keeping dengue fever from reaching epidemic proportions in that country. Brazil, however, was not as fortunate: There the explosion in mosquito numbers caused an increase in dengue fever cases that approached ten times that of the previous year.

Nor is the United States immune to the risks posed by El Niño–driven spikes in the mosquito population. Though malarial mosquitoes do not pose as great a threat in this country as they do in many others, the 1997–98 El Niño nevertheless brought fears of outbreaks of this disease and encephalitis, another mosquito-borne ailment that is potentially deadly.

Hordes of Creeping, Crawling, Flying Critters

The United States, like other countries hard hit by El Niño rains, had more than mosquitoes to contend with in the wake of the 1997–98 episode. Spring and summer 1998 saw a bug boost across the board on the Pacific coast and along the breadth of the American South. It was a bumper season for exterminators but a time of (at least) annoyance for the rest of the folks living in these regions as El Niño lived on after its death in the form of armies of ants, oodles of beetles, busloads of bees, thickets full of crickets, grasshoppers by the hopper-full, tons of termites, wasps by the *Mayflower*-full, and more than enough ticks to make you sick.

More Bloodsucking Parasites

The ticks were, of course, of particular concern. In the spring of 1998 the Lyme Disease Foundation predicted that El Niño was going to be responsible for an increase in the incidence of that tick-borne disease. Since ticks, like mosquitoes, are blood-sucking parasites, they have the potential to spread a number of diseases in addition to Lyme disease, which carries a fever and flulike symptoms at first and can result in chronic arthritis, fatigue, and joint, skin, and nervous system abnormalities. Among the other illnesses commonly spread by ticks are Rocky Mountain spotted fever, which has flulike symptoms; babesiosis, which causes anemia; tick paralysis, brought on by a toxin secreted by ticks while feeding; and ehrlichiosis, marked by fever, lethargy, and lack of appetite.

In El Niño–drenched regions such as the North-west, where the tick population—and incidence of tick-related disease—is relatively high, tick populations did indeed grow markedly in the summer of 1998. But because residents of these areas were already accustomed to the risks posed by the parasite and because doctors there are accustomed to diagnosing tick-borne ailments, the tick plague did not translate into a corresponding spike in the incidence of these diseases. Cases of Lyme disease, for example, were up in the Northwest in 1998 over 1997, but not at a level proportionate to the tick population growth.

In Florida, however, a state that typically has a sparse incidence of Lyme disease, health officials began bracing themselves during the winter deluge for what they knew would be an extraordinarily bad year for the illness. True to predictions, a Florida tick population that had spread to previously unaffected parts of the state after the shake-up offered by Hurricane Andrew in 1992 grew by summer to numbers previously unseen. And, also following the forecast, the boom resulted in a manifold increase in the incidence of Lyme disease. A vigorous public-health educational effort no doubt kept the outbreaks from being even worse.

A Plague of Locusts (Well, Grasshoppers)

Less dangerous but certainly more bizarre than El Niño's harvest of mosquitoes and ticks was the plague of grasshoppers that descended upon the Southwest beginning in mid-April 1998. As Daniel Otte, curator of insects at Philadelphia's Academy of Natural Sciences, put it, "It's quite clear that there's a population explosion going on."

Otte, a respected entomologist, was of course speaking accurately, but even such strong language (from a scientist) seemed quite an understatement. For while Dr. Otte said that there was a population explosion, he didn't mention that literally clouds of the insects had descended upon southern California, Nevada, and Arizona—millions upon millions of grasshoppers. And Otte also left it unsaid that one of the reasons the population explosion was "quite clear" was that the grasshoppers had swarmed into city centers in these states.

In Lake Havasu City, Arizona, they formed a thick, living carpet on city streets that obscured the median lines from motorists' view. In Indio, California, the city courthouse had to be evacuated after it was inundated by grasshoppers. Swarms braved even such major urban areas as Los Angeles and Phoenix. "It's definitely surreal," said Phoenix resident Jennifer Tomkins, "I moved here from New York City last year because I wanted to live closer to nature, but this is a bit extreme. The spookiest thing is how they swarm all over any kind of light at all."

This behavior was, in fact, thought by scientists to be a big factor in drawing away the plague grasshoppers, composed primarily of the common pallid band-wing grasshopper, from their usual grassland and desert scrub habitats to bright population centers. The lights of Los Angeles, it seems, are capable of attracting more than young men and women with stars in their eyes.

Wanted: Pied Piper

Insects, arachnids, and other crawlers were not the only creatures the 1997–98 El Niño left in abundance; the weather event of the century also left those areas it affected with rain with a surfeit of varmints of the scurrying variety. Moisture, rot, early blooms, and the thriving vegetation left in El Niño's wake led to a frightening boom in rodent populations. Rats and mice are, of course, a major health hazard to humans, as they are responsible for spreading—directly and indirectly—all manner of disease.

One of the biggest concerns accompanying the soaring rodent population here in the United States was that doctors would begin to see a corresponding rise in the number of cases of the dread Hantavirus. Hantavirus is a potentially deadly disease in which the lungs' capillary walls break down and begin to leak. Victims can then literally drown in their own blood fluids.

By the beginning of March 1998, field researchers had observed that the population of deer mice—the rodent species that most commonly carries the predominant Sin Nombre strain of the disease—throughout the Southwest had grown markedly (as measured in mice per hectare) from the "high-mouse" mark established in 1993. That year also featured an unusually lush spring that exploded the rodent population. The result was a Hantavirus epidemic in which more than twenty-five people died from the disease.

This time around, greater vigilance kept the death rate well below that of 1993, despite a frightening increase in the number of cases over that recorded in 1993. Through measures such as a special Hantavirus conference sponsored by the Centers for Disease Control and Prevention in Atlanta, doctors were warned to be aware of Hantavirus symptoms when making diagnoses. Public-health warnings also kept people aware of the risk of contracting the virus and how they might mitigate the threat posed by the teeming rodent hordes. Despite the fact that, by the end of February 1998, 178 cases of the disease had been reported around the country in comparison to 48 reported cases in 1993, there were a mere handful of fatalities this time around compared with an over 50 percent mortality rate fifteen years before.

What's Next? The Rattlers Eat the Rats

Disease, as it turned out, was but one of the risks posed by the robust rodent population. As we have seen, El Niño's rains brought an abundance of greenery that in turn fueled the increase in mice and rats. So what did the increase in rodents spur? Why, a jump in the numbers of a species that considers these vermin a tasty little meal indeed: the rattlesnake. Herpetologists (scientists who study snakes and reptiles) noted in early May 1998 that the beginning of the rattlesnake's breeding season, then under way, coincided with the spike in rodent numbers. This meant that newly hatched snakes would find ready food supplies, enabling far more hatchlings to survive than is generally the case. Though the full effect of this increased-rattler food supply had yet to be seen at the time of this writing, those who fear snakes took it as an ominous sign that reports of snakebites (as recorded by the Centers for Disease Control) were up slightly in the late spring. Experts, however, reassured the anxious that snakes do not by nature seek to attack humans and are, as the saw goes, "much more afraid of us than we are of them." Serious threat or no, this last seems at least debatable, given San Diego County Animal Control Department spokesperson Lieutenant Mary Kay Gagliardo's prediction that "By the middle of the summer, [we should] expect to see a lot of little ones."

Having seen how El Niño's rains can create population explosions throughout the food chain, we can only wonder nervously what the boom in rattlesnake hatchings will spawn—an explosion in the birthrate of tough, craggy-faced cowboys, perhaps?

9

Buoys, Satellites, Planes, and Finches: The Scientific Quest to Understand and Predict El Niño

When Sir Gilbert Walker formulated the Southern Oscillation in the early part of the twentieth century, he employed what were then state-of-the-art technology and groundbreaking research methods. Tools for measuring meteorological components such as temperature, atmospheric pressure, and wind speed—the barometer, thermometer, and anemometer, respectively—had existed in reliably accurate form for only about fifty years. And the premise that drove his meticulous sifting through meteorological records from reporting stations in and around the Pacific was at the time highly controversial—that weather events in areas far removed from one another could exert a mutual influence.

As cutting edge as Walker's work was in 1924, when he published his definitive work on the Southern Oscillation (it was widely discredited at the time and only years later were he and his work vindicated), his methods and, more important, the tools he had at his disposal, were extremely limited when compared with what is available to meteorological researchers today. For years before and after Walker's time, scientists had to rely on ocean readings from commercial ships that might record a few measurements during their voyages—temperature, humidity, wind, and current speed—as a courtesy. Even Jacob Bjerknes, gathering data during the 1957–58 El Niño for what he would eventually present in 1969 as the Walker Circulation, was assisted by technologies that were nowhere near the level at which they are today—weather satellites were in their infancy, with the Tiros-class orbiters recently launched and the Nimbus-class orbiters in the prelaunch planning stages; neither had, by the early 1960s, been "trained" to look for signs of an El Niño gathering strength in the middle Pacific.

The same, in fact, could be said of those who studied the 1982–83 El Niño as it unfolded in the Pacific. True, that episode took place at a time when the technologies that have transformed climate research—space flight, the computer, highly sensitive measuring devices—had for some time been available to the research community. But these promising elements had yet to be integrated into the synergistic amalgam that now provides scientists with a remarkably clear, real-time set of readings and forecast models.

As we saw in chapter 3, the ten-year TOGA (Tropical Ocean Global Atmosphere) project, a linked network of sensor-equipped buoys and research vessels, satellites, and computers, was in its initial planning phases at the onset of the 1982–83 episode. By the end of its run in 1995, scientists were left with a much improved picture of how the ocean and atmosphere interact and, thanks to the long 1990–95 episode, of the processes of El Niño itself. They were also left with the infrastructure to develop the ongoing TAO (Total Atmosphere and Ocean) project, TOGA's most important legacy. The 1997–98 El Niño, then, provided a fortuitously timed real-life laboratory in which scientists could apply the advances in instrumentation and the analytical tools that had been developed over several decades and that were now being brought together to work in concert after more than fifteen years of planning and experimentation.

The forecast models produced from TAO data for the 1997–98 El Niño were about as good as anyone had hoped and sometimes even better, according to Vernon Kousky of the National Weather Service's Climate Prediction Center in Camp Springs, Maryland. In fact, the issuance in August of a global forecast for the coming winter was in itself a historical act; that this forecast was for the most part borne out must be regarded as nothing short of astounding. Though we may not have realized it when scientists' predictions of El Niño first made headlines in August 1997, we had just witnessed the beginning of the age of the long-term forecast.

Hubble of the Pacific: The TAO Array

The TAO array lies at the heart of the new technology. It is comprised of approximately seventy ocean buoys in the tropical Pacific, moored where they can best record the fluctuations associated with ENSO, the primary motivation for TAO. TAO employs two different types of buoys, ATLAS buoys and PROTEUS current-meter moorings, equipped with sensors that measure a wide spectrum of oceanographic and meteorological data.

ATLAS moorings, deployed in a grid covering the breadth of the Pacific as bracketed by the Tropic of Cancer and the Tropic of Capricorn, are visually impressive affairs. Buoyed by a bright red and white ring of lightweight material, they rise more than 10 feet above the ocean's surface. Each buoy's multitiered superstructure contains a number of highly sensitive temperature and humidity sensors, and each is topped by an anemometer for capturing the speeds of surface winds.

Like an iceberg, however, an ATLAS buoy obscures

more than it reveals at the ocean's surface. On the immediate underside of each mooring is a sensor for monitoring sea-surface temperature (which, as we have seen, is the key component of an El Niño event); and underneath each is a nylon line mooring it to the ocean floor, as much as four kilometers (about three-and-a-quarter miles) down. Additional temperature sensors are attached to the first 500 meters (about 1,600 feet) below sea level, providing temperature readings at variable depths and enabling scientists to measure the upwelling process and to detect the deep-ocean Rossby and Kelvin waves we encountered in chapter 2. Above the surface, the ATLAS superstructure contains apparatus for recording the data it gleans from the ocean and transmitting it to ARGOS (Atmospheric Research Geosynchronous Orbit Satellites) miles above the earth.

The PROTEUS moorings, deployed strictly along the equator, while equipped like the ATLAS buoys above the waterline, trail a different set of sensors underneath the surface. The primary task of these buoys is to record and transmit data on ocean currents—this is why they are also referred to as current-meter moorings. Clinging to each PROTEUS mooring line are a variety of sensors that measure the dimensions, direction, speed, and temperature of ocean currents in the vicinity of each buoy.

The TAO project is organized and maintained by an international consortium consisting of the United

States, France, Japan, South Korea, and Taiwan. The National Oceanic and Atmospheric Administration (NOAA), part of the United States Department of Commerce, is responsible for carrying out the lion's share of the United States' commitment to TAO. Most departments in the NOAA are in some way involved with El Niño research, monitoring, and prediction. And in addition to its involvement in the TAO project, the NOAA launches new research initiatives, both within the United States and, like TAO, in concert with other nations; monitors the impact of El Niño on the fish population in United States coastal waters; acts to disseminate its findings on the ocean and atmosphere to the government and the public at large; and operates a fleet of research vessels to study the world's oceans and atmosphere.

The NOAA's primary research base for El Niño–related studies, the NOAA Climate Diagnostic Center (CDC), is located in Boulder, Colorado. The CDC studies the nature and causes of climate variations on various time scales, from a month to centuries (using some of the paleoclimatological methods we explored in chapter 3 in concert with the much richer collection of data from recent years). The CDC also explores the short-term climate variations associated with El Niño in the United States, the droughts and flooding we described in chapters 4 and 5. It examines global changes associated with the El Niño–Southern Oscillation as well. Among CDC's stated goals are "to advance the understanding and predictions of ENSO, improve monitoring and descriptions of climate variability, identify major patterns associated with these climate fluctuations on decadal and longer time scales, and investigate the air-sea interaction which causes much of the climate variability."

It is another department within the NOAA, however, that deals directly with TAO: The Pacific Marine Environmental Laboratory, or PMEL, conducts investigations in physical oceanography, marine meteorology, geochemistry, and related subjects. With outposts in Seattle, Washington; and Newport, Oregon; PMEL is directly responsible for the installation and maintenance of the TAO array.

Ka'imimoana: From Hunting Submarines to Deploying Buoys

For buoy maintenance, the NOAA/PMEL uses a ten-year-old converted submarine surveillance ship. In this, the NOAA was a beneficiary of the Cold War's end; it received the nearly new ship when it was decommissioned by the navy as part of an across-the-board scaling down of the U.S. armed forces in the wake of the Soviet Union's disintegration.

The refitted ship, newly christened *Ka'imimoana,* is over 220 feet from stem to stern. *Ka'imi,* as she is known to her intimates, spends a good two-thirds of each year shuttling between TAO moorings, primarily in the eastern Pacific (Japan takes care of many of the same tasks in the western Pacific). In addition to routine maintenance of the ATLAS and PROTEUS moorings, *Ka'imi* is also used for recovery and deployment of the buoys. In the case of errant or damaged buoys (vandalism by fishermen is sometimes a problem), *Ka'imi*'s crew may be called upon to perform all three tasks—recovery of the damaged buoy, deployment of a replacement, and maintenance of the recovered unit.

Buoy deployment is slow, physically demanding work that requires a good deal of patience and attention to detail. Safety concerns must also be attended to, for the task—like all work at sea—is not without an element of risk. First, the anchor and mooring line must be coupled and lowered to the ocean floor. This means waiting for more than three miles of nylon cable to wind out. The process cannot be rushed because to do so could mean tangling the long line around which sensor cables must be entwined. This hand-braiding process begins once the deployment crew reaches its last 1,500 feet of line. When the entire length of the line is at last in the water, it is time to—very carefully—attach the buoy itself, which has undergone last-minute tests and calibrations of its instruments and communication devices. The entire process can take as long as eight hours, depending on weather conditions.

Satellites: Communications and Eyes in the Sky

The TAO buoy array, as we've indicated, uses satellites to communicate its data to weather computers and the humans who run them in places like the Climate Diagnostic Center in Boulder. For this task, TAO employs ARGOS, a satellite-based system that collects, processes, and disseminates environmental data from a variety of fixed and mobile platforms worldwide, including the TAO array.

ARGOS was developed jointly by the Centre National des Etudes Spatiales (CNES, the French space agency), the National Aeronautics and Space Agency (NASA), and the NOAA. The system utilizes both ground- and satellite-based resources to accomplish its mission. This includes instruments carried aboard the NOAA Polar-Orbiting Environmental Satellites (POES), receiving stations around the world, and major processing facilities in the United States and France. This fully integrated system works to locate and deliver data from the most remote platforms—in this case, buoy moorings in the middle of the Pacific Ocean—to earthbound computers and their users, in close to real time.

Each buoy in the TAO array is constantly engaged in collecting the variety of oceanic and atmospheric data we mentioned earlier; it is also continuously transmitting this data to ARGOS satellites. The ARGOS system processes this data, then sends it back to

Earth, where it is received by the NOAA's Pacific Marine Environmental Lab (PMEL) and fed into computers running TAO display software (we'll look at the role computers play in just a bit).

Interestingly, ARGOS is capable of a great deal more than the work required of it by TAO. What makes ARGOS unique is its ability to geographically locate the source of data anywhere on earth. In its work for TAO, this capability is generally underutilized, as the buoys in the array are, as we have seen, fixed more or less in place. ARGOS's ability to locate transmitting objects within several hundred feet on the globe's vast surface is of great use, however, in the data coordination and transmission required by the thousands of drifting buoys the NOAA and various other national and international bodies have set afloat in the world's oceans. These buoys are, like their moored counterparts in the TAO array, equipped with a variety of sensors to measure oceanic and atmospheric variables such as temperature, humidity, and wind speed. Because they are adrift, they also provide an invaluable understanding of ocean currents. Although those buoys adrift in the Pacific (they are scattered throughout the earth's oceans) do not share TAO's primary mission of investigating El Niño, the information they glean from El Niño's home turf inevitably adds to our understanding of the phenomenon. Without ARGOS, coordinating the information gathered for analysis in land-based laboratories would be impossible.

Looking Down on El Niño

The TAO buoy array in the Pacific is but part of an integrated system of sensors that pool their information to provide the world's computers with a constant stream of data. Since the early 1980s, a variety of weather satellites have tracked El Niño events as they have unfolded. As early as the 1960s, however, early-generation weather satellites played a huge role in giving us a global perspective on the weather. In fact, pictures of large, Pacific-spanning cloud systems taken from early meteorological satellites inspired Jacob Bjerknes and convinced him he was on the right track in his search for the Pacific-wide teleconnections that he would eventually formulate into the Walker Circulation.

While buoys are invaluable for the subsurface readings they provide, a satellite can give the big picture literally. The first efforts at mapping sea-surface temperatures and cloud cover from space were conducted with data from NASA's Nimbus series of satellites. Our capacity to monitor sea-surface temperatures from above greatly increased with a new instrument technology, the Advanced Very High Resolution Radiometer (AVHRR), which was first flown on the NOAA's TIROS-N weather satellite launched by

NASA in 1978. It was also subsequently launched aboard the NOAA-6 satellite in 1979. In 1981, an improved version of the AVHRR was launched on the NOAA-7 satellite. The new AVHRR model was able to correct its readings for atmospheric water vapor, something the previous version of the instrument was unable to consistently do. NOAA-7 and the subsequently launched NOAA-9 and NOAA-11, also equipped with the new AVHRR technology, provide researchers—and the computers they use for mapping and running forecast models—with sea-surface temperatures throughout the equatorial Pacific.

The TOPEX/Poseidon satellite launched in August 1992 offers another type of data. TOPEX/Poseidon is, like the ARGOS system, part of a joint U.S.-French research mission to better understand the processes behind El Niño. The satellite, orbiting some 830 miles above the earth, measures sea levels in the Pacific Ocean along a route that is repeated every ten days. Sea-level data have been a part of the search for El Niño's integrated teleconnections since Walker's day; obviously, Walker did not have the ability to track sea levels across a huge swath of the Pacific every ten days. Nor were the readings he received as accurate as those recorded by TOPEX/Poseidon, which uses what is called a dual-frequency altimeter, developed by NASA, to relate the changes in ocean currents that result from the climate changes brought by El Niño. TOPEX/Poseidon data is processed and disseminated by yet another arm of the NOAA, the National Data Center's Laboratory for Satellite Altimetry. The sea-level information gleaned by the satellite is also one of many variables fed into the weekly ocean models run by supercomputers at our National Weather Service.

Joint space ventures between the United States and France aren't the only ones yielding information crucial to the scientific quest for a better understanding of ENSO. In 1996, NASA placed a scatterometer—a device for measuring the speed and direction of ocean-surface winds from space—aboard the Japanese Advanced Earth Orbiting System (ADEOS). Another joint U.S.–Japanese venture, part of NASA's Earth Probe series, was launched in 1997. Called the Tropical Rainfall Measuring Mission, it utilizes both radar and passive microwave detection to provide measurements of clouds, precipitation, and terrestrial radiation processes in the lower latitudes, including that part of the Pacific Ocean where El Niño's warm waters lie.

SeaWIFS Sees the Sea Bloom

A similar satellite research project begun by NASA in the late summer of 1997 is called SeaWIFS (for Sea-Viewing Wide Field-of-View Sensor). Its five-year mission is not to explore new worlds and boldly go where no man has gone before but rather to learn more about our own planet, especially the waxing and waning of phytoplankton growth in the earth's oceans.

Phytoplankton are the microscopic plants that form the foundation of the ocean's food chain. We saw in chapter 2 how El Niño reduces upwelling of cold subsurface water in the eastern Pacific, which in turn reduces the anchovy population in Peru's coastal waters. The anchovy in this area either die or move elsewhere because their primary food source is phytoplankton, the supply of which drops off sharply with reduced upwelling.

During the 1997–98 El Niño, oceanographers involved with SeaWIFS wanted to learn more about how the phenomenon affected phytoplankton growth in the equatorial Pacific. To accomplish this, they focused the SeaWIFS satellite's instruments on El Niño's home turf, Ecuador's Galápagos Islands. The Galápagos, nearly 650 miles off of South America's Pacific coast and directly astride the equator, are situated in the heart of El Niño's hot waters. As such, they are the first land areas to feel El Niño's effects, and the effects are particularly pronounced there.

What oceanographers found was fascinating. As expected, phytoplankton, and a variety of marine life that depend on them, practically vanished with El Niño's onset. But once El Niño ended in May 1998, the turnaround stunned scientists with its suddenness. As NASA oceanographer Gene Feldman told CNN in September 1998—the mission's one-year mark—"Ocean conditions changed very dramatically. . . . Within days, the waters around the Galápagos, hundreds of thousands of square kilometers, just erupted biologically."

Helping Us Sort, Helping Us See: The Role of Computers in El Niño Research

We are living in the information age. Never before have so many facts, so much data, been available to us as a society at large and to scientists seeking to understand the world in which we live. We have indicated throughout this book the vital role computers play in researching the forces at work in the El Niño–Southern Oscillation. Such information-gathering resources as the TAO buoy array and the various "watchful" satellites owe their very existence to the advent of computer technology. And it is computers that help us make sense of the mountains of numbers they provide. Put another way, computers have vastly expanded our capacity to gather and process information. We are also entering an era when computers are helping us see the world in an entirely new way or, perhaps more accurately, when computers are capable of presenting information to us in a way that is more organic to the way the human mind works than are the spreadsheets and tables with which we have come to associate computers.

None of this is to say that human researchers have become in any way superfluous. Feats such as Sir Gilbert Walker's meticulous—and correct—analysis of thousands of pieces of meteorological data from almost as many sources and in a multitude of different forms seem all the more impressive when we consider how much scientists rely on the assistance of computers for managing data. Analysis is still the province of humans; even those sophisticated computers that are able to recognize patterns in sets of data collected from our atmosphere and oceans are still able to recognize only those patterns that a human programmer has taught them to look for.

Computer Modeling: Not Yet Perfect, Never Will Be

In chapter 2 we saw how the near-infinite variables of weather interdependencies necessitated and taxed the abilities of the first supercomputers. As the power of supercomputers has grown, so has our ability to give more accurate—and, as we have seen, more long-term—forecasts. Our ability to successfully "model" the onset of a particular El Niño and the ways in which it will unfold has grown proportionate to our understanding of the many different ways in which it can take hold and manifest itself. We have needed to study El Niño with the sort of intense scrutiny we have brought to bear in the last half of the twentieth century to realize that the "canonical" El Niño is, in many ways, intrinsically elusive. Equatorial trade winds slacken during the buildup phase of most El Niños; in the buildup phase of others, such as the 1982–83 event, they do not. El Niño is characterized by heavy rains and flooding in California; but El Niño can bring severe drought to California, as it did in the 1976–77 event. El Niño lasts several months; and El Niño lasts several years, as it did during the 1991–95 marathon. The list goes on.

We have, however, succeeded in recognizing enough of El Niño's identifying characteristics to come up with a pretty good composite sketch. When computer models, in their extrapolation of what weather will be like tomorrow (and the next day, and the day after that . . .), come across these traits, they can be reasonably certain that they've spotted their culprit, even if certain "canonical" marks of an El Niño are not present. To extend our composite-sketch metaphor, even if El Niño manages to disguise its familiar "nose" (say, the slackening of trade winds at buildup), computer models can recognize it by that distinctive birthmark on its cheek (say, the warming of equatorial waters off the South American coast by at least 3°–5°C).

The real challenge for the computer models lies in getting from the weather events of today to signs they will recognize as being characteristic of El Niño. Medieval thinkers viewed the cosmos as a series of concentric spheres: The earth's orb was contained within a larger sphere, which we saw as the night sky, which was in turn contained within several other spheres of mostly theological significance. All of these spheres, according to medieval thought, turned within each other according to a synchronized logic. Outside of them all was the force that they believed set all the nested spheres into motion, the primium mobile—essentially the hand of God. While we have become increasingly adept at identifying El Niño even in its earliest stages and when given only ambiguous clues, we still search for what, exactly, makes it happen in the first place. We are still searching for El Niño's primium mobile.

We can be reasonably certain that when we do find it, it will not be a single factor but a complex set of them. Herein lies the difficulty. More accurate and abundant data, the computers to crunch these numbers, and a refined theoretical grounding have allowed us to sway along to the rhythm of weather's dance, but we are far from knowing all its steps. And as long as there is an element of chance in the universe, even the best computer models can offer no more than educated guesses.

Computer modeling of the weather will continue to improve as it has since the fifties. Our understanding of how today's weather gives us tomorrow's will increase. We already reap many of the benefits of this constantly improving technology, from the trivial (knowing to bring an umbrella to work the day after tomorrow, thanks to the five-day forecast on the nightly news) to the essential (advanced warning of El Niño for farmers and disaster planners). But until modeling gives us absolutely accurate forecasts—and that day will never come, as close as we may get—we also need observational tools that will enable us to see a gathering El Niño at the earliest possible juncture.

Red Means Hot, Blue Means Cold: A Vision of the Pacific

This is precisely what computers do for us in processing the information we receive from the TAO array and the observational satellites we have discussed in this chapter. Communications technology, abetted by computers almost as much as is information technology, has developed to the point where we can get accurate measurements from the middle of the Pacific, or the upper reaches of our atmosphere and beyond, in real time or very close to it. We can get the data that describe far-away events in numerical form as the events unfold.

Real-time data-reporting is of limited use, however, if the data is presented in purely numerical form. Numbers must be pored over, analyzed with an eye toward patterns that are not readily apparent on the black-and-white of a computer readout. This takes time, the sort of time that makes real-time data-reporting a sort of "hurry-up-and-wait" proposition. So to maximize the potential of data delivery in real time, we need something that will enable scientists to conduct analysis in real time.

When scientists at the NOAA's Pacific Marine Environmental Laboratory look at a computer monitor to see the latest readings from the TAO array, they do not see columns of numbers scrolling down the screen. Rather they see a multicolored map of the Pacific Ocean. The TAO computers are able to map, or visualize, the data they are fed. Temperatures are assigned corresponding colors in a gradation that ranges from ice blue to fiery red. The approximately seventy buoys in the TAO array, as we have said, are laid out in a grid stretching across four thousand miles of ocean and reaching north-south from the Tropic of Cancer to the Tropic of Capricorn. This grid is recreated—superimposed on a map of the Pacific— on the screens of the NOAA computers. Each buoy lends its reading—and the corresponding color—to its place in the grid. The color of the picture as a whole is constantly undulating in response to minute fluctuations in ocean temperature from one moment to the next—this is the real-time component.

The colors displayed by whole sectors of the grid tend to change more gradually, over the course of hours, days, weeks. Regardless of the rate of change, however, the NOAA scientists—and the rest of us, thanks to the Internet—can at a glance see a complete picture of the temperature of the Pacific Ocean. When red means hot and blue means cold, it doesn't take a mathematician or a meteorologist to figure out where it's hot and where it's cold. And when those patches of red begin to grow ever larger in the central and eastern Pacific, it's immediately apparent that an El Niño is under way.

This sort of computer display is available not only for the real-time transmissions of the TAO data, but for that from the satellites we've mentioned in this chapter as well. So scientists can also see visual representations—mapped out—of humidity, wind speed, current, and sea level, either side by side or integrated into a single image. Individual frames in the ever-changing "movie" of the Pacific can be retrieved for comparison with one another or with the current picture. The same can be done with depictions of normal—average—conditions, so as to show deviations from the norm. Computer models of future weather can also be displayed in this fashion in a constant, colorful state of flux in response to the ever-changing stream of data they are receiving from the TAO array and observational satellites. Patterns that would require long hours to discern from a screen full of numbers can be "visualized," in the parlance of this technology, in a moment.

Just as the TAO array provided a fail-safe against satellite readings of sea-surface temperature being fooled by atmospheric interference of the sort we saw in chapter 3, when El Chichon's eruption threw enough volcanic ash into the air to mask the rising

fever in the Pacific, computer visualization offers a
fail-safe against the failure of computer models of the
weather. It performed precisely this function in giving us advance warning of the 1997–98 episode in
May 1997. At that time, the computer model with
the best track record for predicting El Niño was predicting La Niña conditions for the winter of 1997–
98. NOAA scientists knew what they were seeing
unfold, however: a growing patch of red in the cen-
tral-eastern Pacific. The alarm was sounded and we
were given the best lead time yet to prepare for the
event. Meanwhile, to their credit, once the computer
models were fed this new information, they provided
a very good picture of how this particular El Niño
would manifest itself.

Into the Storm: P-3 Flights

If you think that all this high-tech gadgetry has
taken the adventure out of meteorological research,
think again. There's plenty of adventure still to be
had aboard an Orion P-3 turboprop that's flying right
into the teeth of an El Niño–generated storm off the
California coast. CALJET, a NOAA-sponsored program, conducts these flights to learn more about the
massive thunderstorms that track the storm and batter the Californian coast during an El Niño.

When satellite images show that an El Niño storm
is headed toward the West Coast, the P-3s are scram-

bled to intercept it. The flights, manned by about fifteen crew members and atmospheric scientists, are guided to the heart of storms by vehicles referred to as DOWs—Doppler on Wheels. You may recall seeing these vehicles—instrument-laden vans with dish-shaped Doppler weather radar mounted on the roof—in the movie *Twister*; indeed, the DOWs were initially developed for improved tornado tracking.

Each mission is somewhat different from another, but generally the P-3s fly to the storm center and then begin crossing the storm front—the boundary between pressure systems and warm and cool air—at different altitudes. At the same time, a P-3 research team will drop sondes, miniature weather-measuring probes with radio links, so as to get a vertical picture of the storm as well. In an average flight, which can run up to twelve hours, a P-3 will make successively lower passes through the storm and then descend to the very low altitude of about 150 feet over the ocean so as to gather information on air currents nearer sea level.

The P-3 flights are analogous to the TAO array, except that they are "on the go." Just as TAO, by going beneath the surface of the ocean, gives a multidimensional, close-up picture of what's going on in the Pacific that is unavailable from satellite sea-surface temperature readings alone, P-3 research flights get to the heart of a storm that a satellite can't "see." And, like TAO, the way P-3s cross the storm front at various altitudes and drop sondes gives maximal coverage in a gridlike fashion.

Back to the Past: Genetic Clues to El Niño in Darwin's Backyard

High-tech satellites, computer systems, and P-3 flights are not our only tools for studying El Niño, however. The earth's living creatures have witnessed many more El Niños than have humans, and perhaps no creatures on earth have endured these events for so long and as dramatically as have those that inhabit the Galápagos Islands. By studying them, it is felt, we can learn more about El Niño's past and about its effect on the planet's wildlife.

The Galápagos Islands are of course best known for being the place where British naturalist Charles Darwin formulated and researched his theory of evolution in, as fate would have it, an El Niño year. They lie in a region that spawns the storms that batter the South American coast during an El Niño, where the formation of giant convection clouds, storm cells up to thirty miles across, can be witnessed that will then travel east with their cargo of rain. The life on these islands hangs, even in the best of times, in the fragile balance of small-scale ecosystems, where even minute changes in one segment of the biological community can spell catastrophe.

El Niño is not, for the Galápagos, the best of times. The drastic drop in phytoplankton in the surrounding waters, witnessed by the SeaWIFS satellite program, can have a devastating effect on local populations such as sea lions, blue-footed boobies, and flightless cormorants, which all depend on fish that feed on the tiny plants. The marine iguana is also adversely affected by El Niño, which decimates the supply of native seaweed that comprises most of the iguana's diet. All of these animals were hit very hard by the 1982–83 El Niño but less drastically by the 1997–98 episode.

Interestingly, though, the finch that proved such an inspiration to Darwin in forming his theory—and now called the Darwin finch—has found a way to thrive even in El Niño years. Darwin's thoughts on the origins of species crystallized when he realized that the thirteen different species of finch that inhabit the archipelago, distinguished from one another by minute variations in the shape of their beaks, had evolved from a common ancestor in response to the particular food-gathering needs on their respective island habitats. It seems as though the species of finch inhabiting the island Daphne Major has found a way to adapt to the particular food-gathering exigencies of El Niño. Within as little as one breeding season, finch hatchlings greet an approaching El Niño with variations in their beak and body shapes designed to maximize feeding on the vegetation and insects made more plentiful by El Niño's rains and warmth.

This finding, based on more than twenty years of

research by Princeton University scientists Peter and Rosemary Grant, is astonishing for the quickness of the finches' evolutionary adaptation. The rapidity with which the finch meets the evolutionary challenge presented by something as ephemeral as El Niño leads scientists to suspect that the El Niño response is deeply coded in the bird's genetic history, the implication being that El Niño has been with us—or at least the finches—for a very long time indeed. And according to British biologist Robert Bensted-Smith, head of the Darwin research station in the Galápagos, the adaptation proved successful for the finches during the 1997–98 El Niño: "The heavy rains that El Niño brought caused vegetation and insects to flourish all around the archipelago, and this led the finches that feed on them to breed like mad."

It serves as a potent reminder that while humans send machines into orbit around the earth and into the middle of the ocean to understand El Niño, life continues on earth as it has for aeons upon aeons, El Niño or no, oblivious to the frenzied human desire to comprehend and control the forces of nature.

Forecast Disaster?
The Future of El Niño

The El Niño of 1997–98, the "mother of all El Niños," or, if you prefer, the "El Niño of the Century" dissipated in May 1998 and is now history. At the time of this writing, late September 1998, the Pacific Ocean is slowly cooling toward normal, and El Niño's residual effects are with us still. This has allayed somewhat the anxiety spread by forecast models that predicted a plunge straight from El Niño's warm waters into a strong cold phase. In late February, after El Niño had made its belated, furious entrance on the West Coast, the buzz was, as *Time* magazine put it, "If you thought El Niño was bad, wait until you see his sister." So far we have managed to avoid that particular extreme, although computer forecast models suggest that 1999 will bring a moderate to strong La Niña episode.

We have seen the damage, death, and destruction wrought by the 1997–98 El Niño. The bill, in dollars, is still being tallied but is sure to exceed the thirteen billion dollars' worth of damage caused by the 1982–83 episode. Without the months of advance warning we got from the TAO array and the other detection methods we discussed in the previous chapter, the loss of human life would doubtless have been much worse; as it was, the death toll easily approached several thousand, though it is hard to attribute an exact number of deaths to El Niño when so many come from secondary effects such as disease or, in the case of, say, plane crashes, the smoke from forest fires encouraged by El Niño drought. Agricultural losses, too, would have been much greater if not for the early warning and the mitigation efforts it inspired. The toll on wildlife is also difficult to reckon, with some species "winning" and other species "losing" from El Niño's effects, but when rain forests, coral reefs, and their denizens are among the victims, the final reckoning cannot be thought of as anything but grave.

We did dodge some bullets this time. Although Californians would probably be hard-pressed to think of themselves as fortunate in the 1997–98 El Niño, they were spared a good three months of El Niño deluge because of the late onset of the pineapple express—the regime change in the subpolar jet stream that sends moisture from the region of Hawaii straight to the West Coast—resulting in damage that fell billions short of the direst predictions for this El Niño. Perhaps more significant and certainly more terrifying is the near miss Los Angeles experienced with what would have been a historic catastrophe.

On September 12, 1997, a massive hurricane with sustained winds of 185 miles per hour and gusts of over 200 miles per hour sat off the California coast, poised to strike. Ocean temperatures nearing 80°F fueled the storm's fury and, if the computer models were to be believed, were leading Hurricane Linda straight toward Los Angeles. Linda was the strongest eastern Pacific hurricane seen since the advent of meteorological record-keeping and it was making its way toward one of the world's largest urban centers. Los Angeles has only once before experienced winds even in excess of 100 miles per hour, and that was more than 150 years ago, when there was a lot less to lose in that town. At the last minute, Linda passed harmlessly out to sea, leaving Los Angelenos to breathe a very heavy sigh of relief and to contemplate how their city was very nearly blown apart by a disaster novel in the familiar litany for southern California.

Some other, longer-range predictions also failed to materialize—the Southeast did not get the ice storms it had feared (though, as we've indicated, the western part of New York, eastern Ohio, and parts of Canada got a deadly ice storm they had not expected); the Indian monsoon did not fail; and southern Africa was not stricken with the drought it had dreaded. So, and this is a sobering thought, as bad as the 1997–98 El Niño was—and make no mistake, it was, in the context of history, devastating—it actually could have been worse, particularly in the United States, home to the world's most severe weather even in "normal" years. In the wake of the El Niño of the century, with warm Pacific waters that covered a span more than one-and-a-half times that of the continental United States, we are left with questions fraught with a good deal of anxiety.

When Will It Happen Again?

The answer at this point is, of course, no one knows. Even the most ambitious long-range forecasts have not probed this far into the murky future of the planet's climate. El Niño events are generally thought to occur every four-to-seven years, with major events such as the 1982–83 and 1997–98 El Niños occurring every eight to eleven years, though their appearances are by no means regular. The historical evidence shows that they are becoming more frequent—and more severe. In fact, the nine El Niños—two of them (1982–83 and 1997–98) the worst ever—we have experienced in the past decade or so show the phenomenon cropping up with unprecedented frequency. Of course, with reliable records extending back only some 150 years we cannot be absolutely certain that this current spate of El Niños is entirely without precedent. This is one of the puzzles that paleoclimatology, which we examined in chapter 3, seeks to answer.

Betty Meggers, a paleoclimatologist at the Smithsonian Institution in Washington, D.C., believes that the earth may experience a "mega-Niño" every five hundred years or so. Research by archaeologist S. Jeffrey Wilkerson, in Mexico, seems to back up this view. He has excavated the remains of a once-thriving port city on the Gulf coast in the Mexican state of Veracruz that was wiped out by a prolonged period of catastrophic flooding about one thousand years ago.

What's more, Meggers believes we're due for another one, and in her words, "if that happens, it's going to be devastating." The question is, was the 1997–98 event it? Or is the recent epidemic of El Niños basically equivalent to the periodic assault of mega-Niños? It is daunting indeed to contemplate an El Niño that would dwarf the 1997–98 episode.

The Global Warming Puzzle

While we can see that given the available historical context, El Niño events are becoming stronger and are occurring with greater frequency, scientists are somewhat at a loss as to why. One hotly debated theory, echoed by Vice-President Gore in the early months of the 1997–98 episode, has it that global warming has exacerbated the phenomenon.

In recent years a broad consensus has emerged among scientists that the earth has, as a whole, gotten warmer over the past one hundred years, since the beginning of large-scale industrialization and the accompanying burning of fossil fuels. When one examines the century's meteorological records, this conclusion is hard to avoid. Further, 1997 was the warmest year on record, globally.

The consensus falls apart, however, when one approaches the thorny question of how these changes should be viewed against the long, long history of the earth. Geological time spans can make changes that occur over one hundred years seem insignificant. Consider that the earth's climate has undergone any number of changes in its history, only to right itself—the ice ages that have periodically affected our planet are a prime example. Some scientists speculate that the earth may undergo analogous periods of warming. Even if this is the case and the global warming trend is temporary and ultimately self-correcting, it is not a source of much solace, if one takes into account the fact that the ice ages lasted thousands of years.

The degree to which the warming trend will continue into the future is another matter of scientific contention. Many scientists point out that if the current trend does continue, the earth will undergo some fairly dramatic changes even within our lifetimes—a time period that, geologically speaking, is but the blink of an eye. But, as we are talking about the future, there is always room for debate.

Debate rages, as well, over the question of what is to blame for the warming effect. The so-called greenhouse effect, in which it is posited that an overabundance of carbon-dioxide gases in the atmosphere traps the sun's heat as it is reflected back from the earth, has gained increasing acceptance over the last decade or so. But there is wide disagreement over the degree to which human activity is responsible. When viewed cynically, this debate might seem fueled by economic self-interest groups wishing to turn a blind eye toward the problems of industrialization.

Putting these debates aside, however, the fact remains that within the period for which we have reliable records, the earth is getting warmer and El Niño is coming more often and with greater force. Are these trends linked? Tom Karl, the head of NOAA's Climate Data Center, believes that they may be: "We are now seeing indications that the effects of El Niño are amplified by warming."

NOAA scientists stress that global warming does not cause El Niño, a phenomenon that has been with us for aeons. But since the ocean atmosphere interactions that comprise El Niño take place within the larger context of the global climate, the two are, to a degree, inseparable. Severe El Niños such as the 1997–98 episode may even give us an idea of what tomorrow holds in store. D. James Baker, the head of the NOAA, says that NOAA computer modeling "tells us that global warming may first manifest itself in changes in weather patterns. In other words, [the 1997–98] El Niño is a taste of what we might expect if the earth warms. It is a window on the future."

The future, in fact, may be with us sooner than we think. Many scientists believe that the average temperature of the Pacific Ocean has increased by a degree (Celsius) or so in recent years; since El Niño events are measured by the degree to which ocean temperature deviates from the average, the El Niño benchmark may have to be adjusted. Consider, though, that if the ocean's temperature gets to a point where it is consistently 3°–5°C warmer than its present average temperature, El Niño conditions will become more or less the norm, whether or not they are called El Niño.

There are also scientists who discount altogether the notion that global warming makes El Niño worse. Dr. Rob Allen, a scientist in the Division of Atmospheric Research of CSIRO, Australia's federal science agency, analyzed global sea-surface temperature and atmospheric pressure data from the past 125 years and came to the conclusion that El Niño works in concert with two other periodic climate fluctuations linked with El Niño. These fluctuations, which oscillate at longer intervals than the El Niño–South-ern Oscillation, "have probably occurred for thou-sands of years," according to Allen. Spates of severe El Niños, such as have occurred in recent years, are a result of the three trends coinciding with one an-other.

The jury is still out, then, on whether global warming exacerbates El Niño. It is also unclear how much, if at all, El Niño itself contributes to global warming. What does seem clear, though, is that stronger and more frequent El Niños do nothing to ameliorate—indeed, they probably worsen—some alarming overall global weather trends. The sorts of sudden, marked changes in climate associated with El Niño tend to take their strongest toll on fragile eco-systems and endangered species. The species that tend to thrive in El Niño's extreme conditions—pests such as flies, weeds, rats, and mosquitoes—are those that are already outgrowing less hardy species on the environmental landscape.

The 1997–98 El Niño encouraged disastrous fires in rain forests from Indonesia to Brazil. Some envi-ronmentalists maintain that more than four million acres were charred in the Indonesian wildfires, while the Brazilian rain forest, dried out not only from El Niño but from logging and intentional burning on its periphery, lost nearly 15 percent of its acreage in 1997. That which remains is drier than has ever been observed. Many scientists fear that half or more of the rain forest could go up in flames at any time if these conditions persist. The world's rain forests are its crown jewels of biodiversity, with the majority of the earth's species residing therein. They join coral reefs as biologically diverse havens gravely threatened by the forces of El Niño. As Daniel Nepstead, a scientist who has conducted research in the Brazilian rain forest for the Woods Hole Research Center, put it, we're on the edge of catastrophe.

The burning of rain forests does not only threaten biodiversity, however. The rain forests, as we have seen, act as the planet's lungs, converting carbon dioxide to oxygen. They are our last line of defense against the buildup of greenhouse gases and they are disappearing more quickly in part because of the drought El Niño brings to these normally very wet regions. What's more, when vast acreages of forest burn, they release even more carbon dioxide into the atmosphere, simultaneously adding to the problem even as the means to solving it turns to ash.

These are bleak trends, indeed, and El Niño or no, some scientists fear that we may have already passed the point where the effects of these trends are irreversible. Aside from taking steps to greatly reduce the introduction of greenhouse gases into our atmosphere, what can be done?

An Ounce of Prevention . . .

Perhaps the only thing that can be done with respect to El Niño is to continue to hone our early detection methods. As we saw in the previous chapter, we are entering the age of the long-term forecast.

This era in scientific advancement, coinciding as it does with the pronounced El Niño episodes of recent years, has given El Niño research a very large impetus that has translated into an increased governmental funding commitment. A recent cost-benefit analysis by the NOAA on the ten-year TOGA research program that spawned the TAO array found that the annual dollar benefits to agriculture alone ranged from 240 to 342 million dollars, a return on investment of up to 26 percent from just one sector of the economy. In a sign that the message has not been lost on our government, Washington recently committed 18 million dollars to establish an international El Niño research center in New York.

The future will probably also see an ever-growing enhancement of TAO's capabilities, in much the same way that we are constantly launching new and improved satellites to study the earth's weather. Computer modeling will also certainly improve over time. Some other advances that the future might bring to weather detection and prediction include radar-equipped buoys capable of detecting approaching jet streams and storm fronts, and unmanned drone aircraft that could supplant the P-3 flights we discussed in the previous chapter and would enable deeper penetration into storm systems.

As Tom Karl of the Climate Data Center puts it, "Being able to forecast a season ahead will help us if our worst fears about more extreme weather come true. With warning, people can do things to mitigate damage as they did [in the 1997–98 El Niño]." Until now, mitigation efforts have focused on protecting homes and businesses; in the future, perhaps we had better work to mitigate El Niño's effects on the planet itself. As we noted earlier in this book, the Pacific Ocean is thought to have a greater effect on the earth's weather than all the world's rain forests, and El Niño is thought to have a more profound influence than anything but the seasons. It would be a deadly shame if these forces indeed supplanted the rain forests to give earth its last, long hot season.

ACKNOWLEDGMENTS

I want to thank the most patient editor in the world, Jacob Hoye; the beneficent Leslie Schnur and Anita Henry at Dell; my tireless research assistant, Jade Hoye; Veronica de Aboitiz; Vivita; and Dr. Kent M. Ainslie of the United States Peace Corps in the Federated States of Micronesia for their invaluable help in putting this book together.

I'd also like to offer my sincere thanks to George and Betty for all things great and small, Derek and Jamie for a well-timed journal article and a wonderful weekend in Colorado, Hank for much research assistance and moral support, Paul and the real Niño for helping me better understand El Niño's effect on vegetation, Michelle for reports from Hawaii, Gill and Thérèse for fellowship and for letting me take liberties with their computers and office supplies, Wally for research assistance, Jon for a couple of great parties and for years of friendship, Jeffrey for always being ready and willing to help, David for years of support and for pathways smoothed, Jeffé for making sure I had a summer, Dr. George and Lois for a first-hand look at ocean observation techniques, Richard and Carol for years of support and more good meals than I can count, Martha for insights into El Niño's effect on the world's endangered historical monuments, Nug for research assistance and reports from California, Clara for also reporting from the Golden State, Ted and Carol for the groovy Labor Day cookout, Wenonah for the relaxed vibe, Jen for telling me about the grasshopper swarms in Arizona, Cristina for film high jinks and a great pen, Shel for the good vids, Dave and Kara for same—congratulations to both of you, Léna and Patsy for a weight off my shoulders, Jonathon d'E for science help, Meghan for friendship and an open ear, Kathy for her visit during the dog days, Geoff for his constant help, Fitz for some very humorous diversion, and everyone else who gave aid and comfort to me in my state of anomie during the writing of this book. The work is better because of them but the faults remain all my own.